From energizing, inspiring examples of best [illegible] of the worst, stories allow us to experience life from new perspectives and learn from others' mistakes. Stories at Work teaches you to tap into the genuine power of storytelling to increase effective communication, better relationships, and accelerate results. Here Wade moves past theory to offer the building blocks of transformative storytelling for the workplace.

Stephen M. R. Covey, author of the *New York Times* and *Wall Street Journal* bestseller *The Speed of Trust*

In contrast to the explosion of electronic communication and expansive social media networks there is a resurgence among today's organisations and business leaders in the ancient art of storytelling. It is essential that today's leaders have the ability to tell the right story at the right time in the right way in order to get real business results in the rapidly-changing world of the 21st century. How timely then is the publication of this practical guide to organisational storytelling. Comprehensive yet immediately applicable, this very practical guide will prove to be a valuable resource for all managers.

Ken Lee, MBA Director, AUT University

Communication is key in any business – it largely determines (fairly or unfairly) the quality of leadership in organizations. Storytelling is a fundamental facet of communication, and this book practically illustrates this. People remember stories, particularly personal experiences. A really good read. Well done, Wade.

Wayne Besant, CEO, AIA New Zealand

Well done on writing a practical book on how stories at work is one the most critical communication skills of a leader. This book is a great tool for team leaders to develop their communication skills to engage their people, a skill central to business growth.

Chris Bayliss, Executive General Manager of Retail, National Australia Bank

There is a wonderfully subtle and clever blend of art and science, head and heart in this book. In our business we really understand how valuable this blending can be - the artful merging of 'money and magic' is at the center of our business at Fahrenheit in New York, as we create ideas and translate dreams into profitable enterprises and products. Wade shows us how our complex psychologies respond far more powerfully when both our passions and our reason are awakened.

Bridget Liddell, Managing Principal, Fahrenheit 212

The art and impact of storytelling in the corporate environment is expounded in a concise and compelling way. Wade Jackson uses his considerable experience and that of others to illustrate this business tool with splendid examples.

Nevil Gibson, *The National Business Review*

True story: Wade Jackson, off-the-cuff artist, tycoon trainer and serial storyteller, phoned in October and asked if I would write a few impressions of his book. I said I'd be delighted. He emailed in November, and reminded me gently in December. He called again before Christmas – three times – and some more in January. Too many times to remember, actually, but Wade is a helluva nice guy. Persistent, too.

So I read 'Stories at Work'. It was great. Long enough to be useful and short enough to be entertaining. Telling a story well is a generous and personal act, and Wade works on getting the character through. He's also good at reminding us to listen, and even to be silent. I liked that. And he tells stories through the text: tall tales, quips and anecdotes, from Carl Jung to Don Johnson. He wraps it up with some short interviews with business people who have used storytelling on their way to becoming big cheeses.

And then I sat on this review for another week, trying to work out how it ends. But I realised it's not like that; it's what you do with the book that counts. I have no doubt 'Stories at Work' will change many careers, and perhaps a few lives. So buy Wade's book and find out how your story ends.

Matt Cooney, *Idealog Magazine*

Stories
at Work

A practical guide to
organisational
storytelling

Wade Jackson

Dear Michael

much love!

W

Wade Jackson
P.O. Box 56-263
Dominion Rd
Auckland 1446
New Zealand

Designed and produced by:
Pindar NZ
209 Great North Road, Grey Lynn,
Auckland 1021
New Zealand
www.pindar.co.nz

Printed in New Zealand

ISBN 978-0-473-18319-6

Contents

Dedication

This book is dedicated to my Mum, Kaye, and Dad, Don. Thank you for providing me with so many wonderful stories. Except the youth camp, Mum – I'm still scarred. And the electrocution, Dad – nice try.

Acknowledgements

I'm so grateful for the art of improvisation, an art form that has given and continues to give me so much, has helped shape who I am and provides me with laughter every day. Thank you to Michael Robinson, the person who taught me so much about performing improv. Thank you to The Improv Bandits, past and present, for being a great bunch of guys who help keep me sane.

I'm grateful for all the workshop participants over the last 16 years who have taught me equally as much and allowed me to hone my craft.

A special thank you goes to all the people who I interviewed for this book and those who assisted with the interviews. They so generously gave me their time and I truly appreciate their interest and the efforts they made in contributing to this book. I acknowledge and thank:

Steve Bayliss, General Manager of Marketing, Air New Zealand
Roger Bell, CEO, Vero Insurance
Marie-Ann Billens, Managing Director, Estée Lauder Companies
Bob Harvey, Mayor of Waitakere City
John Harvey, Partner, Price Waterhouse Coopers
Dick Hubbard, Chairman of Hubbard's Foods and former Mayor of Auckland
Brent Impey, CEO, Media Works
Murray Jack, CEO, Deloitte
Cath Lomax, Head of Sales and Service, ANZ
David Pearce, CEO, CanTeen

Kevin Roberts, Worldwide CEO, Saatchi & Saatchi
Michelle van Gaalen, Group Manager Retail, NZ Post

Thank you to Catherine Love from ANZ, Liam McGee from Deloitte, Rose Caughey and Christina Livingstone from Estée Lauder for assistance with the interviews.

Thank you also to Leigh Cattin, who so wonderfully transcribed all the interviews, and Julie Kennedy, who did a tremendous job of editing this book. A special thank you to the great storyteller Mike Hutcheson for writing the foreword.

And finally, my gorgeous wife Evie, my daughter Sabina, my son Axel, you are my favourite people and partners in play. You are wonderful travel buddies, and what a ride it is!

Foreword

It's been said that the thing that separates humans from other living creatures is the opposable thumb. Use of these clever digits is deemed to have enabled us to achieve all kinds of dexterous feats which, over millennia, have meant we can laud it over the rest of the animal kingdom – and indeed, rule the world.

Personally this seems too simplistic. It's more likely the real reason behind our dominance lies in the ability to tell stories. By being able to tell stories – and organisational stories at that – we have learned to coordinate and galvanise collective action for common purpose.

By contrast, if other species such as fish and insects (which both outweigh humankind by at least 20 to 1) could talk, they could gang up and kick us off the planet because of the way we're treating it. With that kind of dominance in terms of biomass, they would swamp us. The sharks would eat those of us brave enough to enter the water and the termites and wasps could rally and sting the landlubbers to death.

Stories enable us to make sense of our lives and are an essential ingredient of successful leadership. Professor Howard Gardner, noted Harvard psychologist, educator and author of *Leading Minds*, says,

> ... the basic point is that leadership involves the creation of powerful narratives that are much more than mission statements or messages. They are actually stories where there are goals and obstacles, where good and bad things can happen along the way and where the people involved feel part of an enterprise that's trying to end

up in a better place. In order for a story to be effective in the long run, though, it must be 'embodied'. The individual or institution that bears the narrative must behave consistently with it. Because if you tell one story and live another – if you don't walk the talk – to use the vernacular – then the story doesn't have appeal.

In *Stories at Work* Wade has written a remarkable little book – and I say 'little' advisedly, because it doesn't take lots of words to impart fundamental truths. In fact many books should really be essays. They are turned into books by publishers who can't get their heads around 'less is more' and don't see anyone paying good money for 'short thoughts'. Maybe the advent of the Kindle and the iPad will start a whole new trend in book–buying?

The thrust of this book lies in the first five chapters – the 'Why? What? When? Where? and How?' of storytelling. These insightful and fundamental principles are brought to life through the practical and often inspirational stories of notable men and women who articulate and amplify these principles.

Wade has made great use of his experience, as an Improv actor, trainer and master storyteller himself, to create a clear and simple exposition about how we can create stories and bring meaning to our own lives and organisations.

Mike Hutcheson
Author of *Relax and Grow Rich*
January 2011

Introduction

Wherever there is culture and values there are stories. It's as true for communities as it is for organisations today. I wanted to inform you as leaders how to use storytelling within your organisation and to share the techniques with you. I refer to this as organisational storytelling. This book grew out of two desires. As a trainer and consultant, I found myself spending the first few hours of my sessions covering the basics of organisational storytelling. I wanted to be spending more time helping people craft their stories and working at becoming better storytellers, yet it's essential to give the context of the work. When leaders have a tool they are confident in using then positive change will occur.

I also wanted to provide a quick guide that summarised the work without getting into too much detail. It was obvious that the topic resonates with people as participants kept asking for a resource they could dip in and out of at will and stay fresh, inspired, and on track. In order to create a book that leaders could use, it had to be concise enough that they'd want to keep it on their desk. Winston Churchill's famous comment reminded me to keep the book short and therefore practical: 'This report, by its very length, defends itself against the risk of being read'.

So, my intention in writing this book is two-fold. To provide you, the busy executive, leader, manager with a simple and practical how-to guide for using the power of storytelling in your professional life. And to accelerate the positive impact organisational storytelling can have for your organisation.

I have drawn liberally from a range of areas such as psychology, neuroscience, organisational development and best business practice and of course the art of improvisation, to provide an overview of the why, what, when, where and how of organisational storytelling and putting the theory of it into practice. What I also wanted to provide was real stories and knowledge from leaders who use storytelling personally and in their organisations. The few books available on organisational storytelling lack this practical component and of course, it is their stories that will stick in your mind.

Those in a leadership role walk the tightrope of balancing their time between inspiring their team, getting buy-in for ideas, implementing strategy, managing tasks, building relationships, coaching others and a whole myriad of other demands. If you focus your attention solely on one area for too long, you'll soon find yourself off-balance and falling off the wire. The one element that all these demands have in common is – communication.

And this is the essence of this book. These days in business, being an effective communicator isn't a 'nice-to-have' – it's a 'must-have'! Master storytelling and you will be a more effective communicator and enjoy success in meeting work demands. Being a more effective communicator means you and those around you will become more productive and achieve better results. You will have more control of your destiny, and living in a time where rapid, constant change is the norm, having that control gives you peace of mind.

Stories are like oxygen – they are all around us and provide us with a life force every moment of our lives yet we rarely notice them or pay them much attention. Take them away and we die. We need stories, not just our own but those of others too. It is through the telling and sharing of stories that we make connections which help us understand who we are and make sense of the world around us.

Every culture has a history of storytelling. You have a wealth of storytelling knowledge stored unconsciously as this natural storytelling skill is in your genes. The purpose of this book is to help you tap into this knowledge, to make it conscious and give you a few tools that you can practise storytelling with. With practice, the knowledge will become a part of you that you will be able to draw upon unconsciously at work and at home.

You are the writer and actor of the most important story of all – your life. You're probably the producer too – financially responsible for your story.

Like any good story, your life has a beginning, middle and an end. Every day through the choices that you make, you write a little bit more of your story. What you do now, today, helps shape the rest of your story.

By choosing to read this book and following its tips, you are choosing to invest in making your life more fun, more connected to others and more purposeful.

I hope you enjoy this adventure into the world of organisational storytelling and wish you a happy ever after.

WJ

Part I
The Theory

1: The Why

» Why use storytelling as a leadership tool?
» Why use organisational storytelling?

Why use storytelling as a leadership tool?

Stories are the number one way we learn and experience the world

Our brain is a storytelling machine. Give it a couple of random, non-related facts and our brain can create a connection quick smart. It may not be the connection you wanted people to get but they will make one regardless. Our brain is a self-organising, pattern-seeking device that creates a narrative out of everything that we see, hear, touch, smell and taste. This ability helps us survive and this ability means our brain is constantly looking for meaning.

Facts and figures don't have any meaning unless there's a story to give it context. The statistic that customer satisfaction has improved by 26% doesn't mean as much to people as the story of one happy customer and the impact the service had on them. People will take their own meaning if you just give them facts so the story you tell frames the facts for them. Your stories help get people on the same page and give them a sense of direction.

We may *think* we make our decisions based solely on logic and reason but we simply use this logic and reason to justify the decisions we've made mainly based on emotion and the stories we tell ourselves. We are rationalising beings rather than rational beings and logic has little to do with the big things in life, from choosing the partner to spend our life with through to choosing which leaders we follow.

> *The heart has its reasons of which reason knows nothing.*
>
> Blaise Pascal

Storytelling is a whole-brain activity

When you hear or share a story, you activate your whole brain. You have to pay attention. Ever turned on the television halfway through a show and tried to follow what's going on? Your brain is furiously trying to make connections so it can understand the plot. You require your memory to keep a track of things and both hemispheres are activated when the language and the emotional centres of your brain are in use, you're reading facial expressions, gestures, and reactions.

You integrate all this information with your intuition; the silent knowledge that resides in your unconscious and as a whole turn it into a meaningful experience – it makes sense to you. You may not be able to explain it, but you know. That's why trying to deconstruct a story is a little bit like dissecting a frog in science class. In trying to understand how the frog works, we kill it and it isn't ever going to be the same again.

Stories have an emotional, psychological and biochemical appeal

Stories engage you on all levels – physically, intellectually, emotionally and spiritually. Stories create emotions and experiencing emotions is at the core of being human. The mind and body are two sides of the same coin. You can't affect one without affecting the other. Someone tells you a story with a happy ending and you feel good. There's a rush of neurotransmitters (brain chemicals) such as serotonin and dopamine that make you feel good. Storytelling therefore induces natural, positive drugs.

Conversely, someone tells you a negative story and it puts you on high alert. We are a survival species and our autonomic nervous system's 'fight or flight' response kicks in. That's why we are attracted to bad news. It's simply a survival strategy. The bad news allows us to use our imagination and prepare ourselves if we find ourselves in that situation. Stories like that make us ask ourselves the question – What would I do?

Sigmund Freud's Pleasure Principle made famous the idea that all our behaviour is motivated by two things: the avoidance of pain and the gaining of pleasure. The stories we hear and tell help guide our behaviour and that of others.

Stories help us remember

Your brain has to compress experiences and information so it can store it as a memory because having the whole experience stored would take up too much space. In order to understand something we like to simplify it, take out the randomness and put it into the form of a story. Every time you remember something you re-create it using different parts of your brain so the act of remembering is actually an act of creative re-imagination. This means that memories are living things, not fixed and constant, but will change depending on your mood, beliefs and new information. Your memories then are stories that summarise experience.

When you hear new information in the form of a story it has much more impact, it has 'stickability' and is therefore easier to remember.

Stories personalise all experience

When you tell a story you are giving your audience (be it of one or one thousand) the opportunity for them to personalise your story for themselves. They interpret your story as it relates to them. This makes storytelling a very collaborative process as they start thinking about what you're saying and how it applies to them.

Since becoming a parent I have a much stronger compassionate reaction when I hear stories about harm coming to a child. Why? Because when I hear those stories, I personalise it – what if that was my child? As a result of this, I'm more compassionate – not the other way round.

Stories allow us to time travel. Telling stories can take us back to a time in the past or to a time in the future. When you hear a story of the past, your imagination places you in that time. When someone paints a picture of the future, you see it in your mind and when that happens, their story becomes your story.

Storytelling is a natural talent we all possess

The beauty of storytelling is that it's an innate skill. You grew up hearing and sharing stories every day of your life. As children we learn that if an ugly duckling can turn into a swan then so too can we develop and find our place in the world. If a small child can stand up to a wolf and survive, then there's hope for us to be brave and surmount the obstacles we meet on our path.

You still do hear and share stories every day, but it's just such a natural way of being that you take it for granted and probably don't consider it storytelling.

Stories are all around us. Turn on the TV, open the newspaper, go to a film, pick up a book, telephone a friend, ask a loved one how their day was or talk to a child and you'll

get stories. They are the means for expressing the human experience. It's how we think, communicate, remember and know ourselves. To be human is to be a storyteller and a story listener. And as in most disciplines, natural talent isn't enough by itself. To be a good oral storyteller, it takes practice.

Why use organisational storytelling?

'Thou shalt not', might reach the head, but it takes 'Once upon a time', to reach the heart.

Philip Pullman

There are many benefits and applications of using storytelling as a tool. But the main idea is that stories connect. They connect people to people and people to ideas. There are many different types of people and types of relationships just as there are many different types of ideas. Storytelling connects us all. Here are eight key areas where storytelling can greatly benefit leaders.

Aligning purpose

Not all leaders are managers, but all managers are leaders. In today's business world, everyone needs to be a leader even if it's just a leader of yourself. Gone are the days of employees being drones who just clock in and clock out after a day's work. Organisations need to tap into each and every employee's heart and soul and set it alight. The way they do this is through story. Every human being seeks meaning and it is through stories that we find meaning. We all want to be a part of something that is bigger than ourselves.

Organisations can offer this to people, to be a part of something that is great. Leaders must tell the story of the organisation's purpose, its mission, its very reason for being and tell it often.

This is the true joy in life, the being used for a purpose recognised by yourself as a mighty one; the being thoroughly worn out before you are thrown on the scrap heap.

George Bernard Shaw

21

Marie-Ann Billens, Managing Director of Estée Lauder, tells a story about the founder of the company to illustrate to her staff the importance of perseverance and creative thinking.

Mrs Estée Lauder was unsuccessful in getting her product into the Gallery La Fayette in France. So she walked through the store and dropped a bottle of 'Youth Dew' on the marble floor. The store had so many people asking what fragrance it was, where could they buy it, when could they buy it, and they had to say no they didn't carry it. Of course the French thought Americans couldn't make fragrance but they had to eat their words and say yes we will stock your fragrance and as a consequence Mrs Lauder was recognised as a 'nose' by her French fragrance foundation, I think she was the first non-French or non-European person to be recognised internationally as a nose – somebody who could create fragrance.

Setting a vision

The organisation's vision is the reality it would have if the organisation achieved its purpose. It is this desired reality that makes people get up in the morning and want to come to work. It's not the vision statement but rather the story behind the statement. To be a $5 billion company might excite those whose bonuses are tied into meeting that target but it's not going to get John and Mary excited each morning and have them put their heart and soul into their work. A story needs to be told to create a shared vision within the team and within the organisation.

Building a culture

An organisation's culture is often described as 'the way things are done around here' but that is an overly simplistic definition. Culture is a dynamic interaction of shared beliefs, values and behaviour that creates meaning for people. Storytelling is the way to expose beliefs, both resourceful and limiting ones, the way to reflect, reinforce and embed values, and the way to demonstrate desired behaviour within the organisation.

Implementing strategy

Strategy is the goals, objectives and action plans that bring about the vision so the organisation is achieving its purpose. When it comes to managerial responsibilities like planning, organising and controlling, again storytelling plays an important role. Stories help us remember and without memory, knowledge is redundant. Stories help people make sense of the constant change organisations face today. There's a reason that strategy follows culture here, because it does in your organisation too. Culture is much more important than strategy. Organisations that merge may have a great strategy but if the cultures clash then the merger will fail to add value. And 83% of the time, mergers do exactly that.

Inspiring and influencing
When a story is told, it is retold in the mind of the people listening to it. If it is a story that gives them hope, purpose, something to aspire to, then they retell it again, this time in their heart. It becomes their story.

There are always two sides to every story so if your story goes against what is already known or expected, then expect push back. Don't try to convince people with facts and statistics. Facts can never compete with the internal story that the people are telling themselves. You have to tell another story that opens them up to the possibility of a different narrative, a different outcome, a different way of being. The key is to tell a story that connects people's needs and wants to your desired outcomes. If you tell a story that answers the question What's In It For Me? (WIIFM), then you are more likely to enjoy success.

No one likes being told what to do or being told what to think. We didn't like it at the age of two and certainly don't like it as adults. Influencing by story is the indirect route. It bypasses direct confrontation and allows the listener to interpret or reinterpret the circumstances for themselves.

The brain thinks by association. When you think of the word *red* – what do you associate it with? Love, blood, wine, stop sign, matador cape and so on. When you tell a story, this results in people associating other stories with it and sharing them and being a good story listener plays a major role in influencing people. Being genuinely interested in other people and listening to their stories will make you influential as people appreciate being heard.

Creating and maintaining relationships
Gossip and sharing non-essential personal information in the form of stories

makes up 60% of our language production, which highlights its importance in maintaining relationships.

When you tell a story you reveal yourself. People see your values, your character from the things you do and the stories you tell. Allowing yourself to be vulnerable takes courage and people respond positively to it. In organisations there is a lot of fear – fear of being wrong, fear of failing, fear of being judged. The higher up you go in an organisation, the more you feel you must always look like you know all the answers. Self-revelation through stories breeds intimacy, which creates and maintains a strong connection with people whether they are team members, colleagues or customers.

Sharing knowledge to coach and upskill

Using stories to help coach and develop people's skills keeps them engaged and open to learning. You can use stories to reframe the way people look at a situation or help them set personal and professional goals.

Put together people not liking their mistakes being corrected along with stories being the number one way we learn, and it makes sense to use more stories when it comes to coaching, upskilling, giving performance reviews, challenging unacceptable behaviour and helping to break down the silo mentality within different departments.

Simplifying communication

Stories communicate on many levels – intuitively, emotionally and holistically. Intuitively is when people relate directly to your speech and gain insight because of their own experience, often without being aware of how this happens – it's unconscious knowledge. Emotionally is when the speaker appeals to people's feelings and holistically is where the speaker makes complex ideas understandable. Across the board, telling stories makes your information more memorable and thereby increases the chance of your message getting across. Story cuts through the information overload that's on offer today. We don't need more information – we're drowning in information. What we need is meaning. We are teleological beings – we need meaning, and a sense of purpose in our lives. If you're presenting to five people around a table or to five thousand in an auditorium, stories are the key for engaging people, giving them meaning and getting them to remember you and your message. End of story.

Summary
Why use storytelling as a leadership tool?
» Stories are the number one way we learn and experience the world
» Storytelling is a whole brain activity
» Stories have an emotional, psychological and biochemical appeal
» Stories help us remember
» Stories personalise all experience
» Storytelling is a natural talent we all possess

Why use organisational storytelling?
» Aligning purpose
» Setting a vision
» Building a culture
» Implementing strategy
» Inspiring and influencing
» Creating and maintaining relationships
» Sharing knowledge to coach and upskill
» Simplifying communication

2: The What

» What are stories?
» Think FIVE: What are the main organisational stories leaders need to be telling?
» Use CLEAR: What are the five rules of narrative?

What are stories?

There are many different definitions of a story and I'll throw mine into the mix. Stories are a sequence of events that progress towards an ending where someone or something has undergone change.

The ancient Greek philosopher Aristotle told us over 2000 years ago that every story has a beginning, middle and an end. The person or object at the end of the story has made some sort of transition by the end of the story.

A story is not just a sequence of events by itself. If you say, 'John rang a former customer and asked them why they switched to the competition', this is not a story. Without there being any change it simply highlights the order of the character's actions. However, by adding a transition to the sequence of events, it becomes a story. John rang a former customer and asked them why they had switched to the competition, was able to rectify the problem and as a result won back the customer's business – now that's a story a manager can use to build on to educate others.

E.M. Forster, author of *A Passage to India*, illustrates the difference between a story and a sequence of events. 'To say "The king died, and then the queen died" is not a story. To say "The king died, and then the queen died of grief" – now that is a story.'

There are many different types of stories – analogies, anecdotes, proverbs, fables, folktales, myths and legends, fairytales, parables, historical stories, even some jokes can be used as appropriate stories. Although these types of stories can be very useful to the leader, they aren't the focus of this book. The purpose is to show the power of organisational storytelling – stories that are more personal to the company, serve a purpose and can be used at work on a regular basis. However I do touch upon these other types of stories in Chapter 4.

There are two elements to stories you need to be aware of: advancing and extending. Advancing is when you move a story forward in plot. Extending is when you add colour to the story, flesh out the detail to paint a richer picture. Using E.M. Forster's example of a story above, the queen dying of grief after the king dies is advancing the story as it moves it forward. To describe the queen, what she was like, what she looked like and how she actually died would be extending the story. In organisational storytelling, you don't always have to do a lot of extending although certain types of stories do benefit from this.

Think FIVE

What are the main organisational stories that leaders need to be telling?
F = Future stories
I = Identity stories
V = Values stories
E = Engagement stories

Future Story
There are two main types of future story.
1. Vision story
2. Call to action story

Vision story
The vision story communicates just that – the organisation's vision, purpose or mission. Its goal may be to inspire people, to get buy-in or give people purpose.

The key for the vision type of story to be successful is to think 'big picture'. This means you need to be artfully vague. The reason for this is that people will have different reasons for working for the organisation. A big picture encompasses all these different reasons. When setting a vision, it needs to be vague enough that people can take ownership of it and make it relevant to them and their role in the organisation. This is the way it becomes a shared vision.

Think of storytelling as painting a picture instead of taking a photograph.

Donald David

By keeping a future story vague you allow for any changes that will develop along the journey. It would be foolhardy to spell out a crystal clear future as no-one knows what the future holds. When something happens that forces a change from the communicated ideal, people will lose trust at best and become cynical at worst. This results in having a lot of negative stories floating around the organisation.

Walt Disney's Vision Story for Disneyland

The idea of Disneyland is a simple one. It will be a place for people to find happiness and knowledge. It will be a place for parents and children to spend pleasant times in one another's company, a place for teachers and pupils to discover greater ways of understanding and education. Here the older generation can recapture the nostalgia of days gone by, and the younger generation can savour the challenge of the future. Here will be the wonders of Nature and Man for all to see and understand.

Disneyland will be based upon and dedicated to the ideals, the dreams and hard facts that have created America. And it will be uniquely equipped to dramatise these dreams and facts and send them forth as a source of courage and inspiration to all the world.

Disneyland will be something of a fair, an exhibition, a playground, a community centre, a museum of living facts, and a showplace of beauty and magic. It will be filled with the accomplishments, the joys and hopes of the world we live in. And it will remind us and show us how to make those wonders part of our lives.

Think of Barack Obama's 2009 presidential acceptance speech where he talked about rebuilding the United States of America. He didn't specifically state how this was going to happen but simply painted a picture of the ideal and reminded people that 'Yes, you can do it'.

Call to action story

A call to action story is used to get a group, team, division or the whole organisation to move in a certain direction. If your desire is to call people to action whether it's to reach new sales targets or embrace a change management process then you'll need a different kind of story. A call to action story requires that you are specific about the desired change you want. Remember people personalise stories and you want this call to action to become their story – not yours! You'll need a story that communicates the basic idea and then lets the imagination of the listeners fill in the detail. So more advancing of the story is required here and not so much extending.

I did some creativity work with the corporate banking section of a large Australasian financial institution. Three teams had to come up with a different idea each and pitch it to their senior managers. One idea was to do 'The Big Lunch' to help enhance communication between the different areas of the business unit. It would be a lunch meeting where members of the team would come together and go for an inexpensive lunch that they would pay for themselves. There was to be no set agenda, they would simply talk over lunch about what was happening in their part of the bank. To make sure people would show up they had a wild card – a senior executive would be there and it was an opportunity for them to have that face-to-face time. Having the idea was only part of the project. They then had to communicate and sell this idea to their senior managers.

They talked about different ways they could present the idea. To me it was obvious what they had to do. They had to tell all the senior managers to get out of their chairs and then take them down to a nearby café and actually have 'The Big Lunch' so they could experience it for themselves.

The team was very nervous about such a move – was this going to be one of those career-limiting actions? To their credit they did it. And the response from the senior managers was amazing. As they sat there with their suit jackets off, eating their sandwiches, they were all sharing ideas about how they could run these types of meetings across the bank and were living the very essence of the idea. This episode in turn became a story within the organisation about the importance of taking calculated risks and nurturing ideas.

A person's imagination fills in and leaves out detail indiscriminately. If you provide the positive frame around a change initiative and encourage people to see for themselves how this change will benefit them, their minds will do the rest and all of a sudden your story has become their story.

People trust the familiar and distrust the unknown. They do not like change. It's a basic survival mechanism that isn't going to be overridden any time soon. Few people enjoy the chaos change brings so try to avoid change at all costs. Because their imagination projects their present situation on to the future, you have to tell a story where a similar change has taken place and worked. Then it becomes acceptable to them.

It's like taking a child to school for the first time. They need to be taken to the school a few times before they start, see a classroom, hear the parent's talk enthusiastically about school so they can assimilate the concept of going to school as a familiar and therefore welcome idea. They need to be able to imagine themselves enjoying going to school. It's no different when you are promoting change in an organisation. Your call to action story helps people assimilate the change idea and make it their own.

Summary
A vision story requires that you:
» Set a positive future scenario
» Be artfully vague
» Be authentic

A call to action story requires that you:

» Be specific about the desired change – not too much detail
» Look for previous examples where it's worked
» Provide a happy ending

Identity stories

There's a saying that goes: 'People don't care how much you know until they know how much you care'. This is the crux of identity stories – they show people who you are. You can have the best strategy in the world, with all the best reasons, but if people don't know you and don't trust you then it's all for naught. People may give all sorts of reasons as to why they didn't do what you asked, or why they didn't take on the new initiative. They may rationalise it but in most cases it boils down to a lack of trust.

If you want to influence people, they have to know who you are. Self-revelation breeds intimacy. If you share a story about yourself, you are taking that person or audience back to that time and they get to see you with their own eyes through the power of their imagination. It's as if they were actually there with you at that time. The beauty is that with identity stories, you select what part of yourself you want to reveal. If you want your team to know that you're open to ideas then share an experience where you walked this talk. You can extend your stories here more. Detail makes the stories come alive so that they transport the audience back to that time and become a kinaesthetic experience. In their mind they actually travel to that time and place and relive the story with you.

I did some presentation coaching with a person who was a very successful foreign currency trader for a bank. So successful that he had been bankrolled to start up his own trading company. He was going to go around and do small presentations to people to get them to invest in his company. When he came to me he had the standard PowerPoint presentation with a lot of information about the company's structure, operations and financial forecasts. I asked him if he'd ever seen the TV show *Dragon's Den* where entrepreneurs pitch their idea for a business to wealthy business people who are looking for an investment opportunity. The reinforcing message that comes from that show is that people invest in people not the company. The wealthy business leaders would say things like, 'I like your idea but I don't like you, so I'm out' or 'I don't like the idea but I want you to come work for me'. He had to let these people know who he was.

So I got the trader to tell a personal story about how he got to where he is now. He told the story about how as a young boy all he ever wanted to do was become an airforce pilot. He became dux of his school, head prefect, captain of the First XV rugby team – achieving all these things so he could become a fighter pilot. He fulfilled his dream until a neck injury playing rugby meant he had to stop flying. He then got into banking and did that for ten years until he headed up the foreign currency trading unit. Now he was starting out on his own.

This story did two things: it relaxed him, as he felt at ease just telling his story and he avoided becoming the presentation robot that many people become when speaking in public. Plus it showed these potential investors that he was a driven, achievement-orientated person who had a burning desire to succeed in whatever he did. The kind of person you'd want to give your money to, to invest. At his first presentation to seven people, six invested. One person invested $10 million. And this story taught me that perhaps I should have been charging commission!

Storytelling is indirect. The trader didn't stand there and tell the audience he was driven and liked to succeed. It wouldn't influence people if he had done that and he didn't need to. His personal story did that for him. The key for an identity story to have an impact is that it must be true. You must be authentic and if you can fake that – you've got it made! Joking aside, if people find out or even suspect you're being manipulative then pack your bags and go home – you won't be leading or influencing anyone.

Summary
» Look to your past for stories – times you've overcome challenges, important lessons you've learned, people who had a positive influence on you, positive and negative childhood memories, the impact your family have had on you
» Be authentic – you have to walk your talk
» Make sure your story is relevant

Values stories
An organisation's values are abstract concepts based on what the organisation deems worthy. These values become concrete concepts through the stories people tell in the organisation. It is through these values stories that an organisation's culture is built, shared and passed on to future generations of employees.

David Pearce, CEO of CanTeen, tells a story about his organisation's values being lived.

> One of our CanTeen values is 'Live Life'. I was at a CanTeen event recently and there was a little man in the audience who I met around this time last year on my first week in CanTeen. When I met this young man 11 months ago he was a tiny wee fellow, still in chemotherapy, bald as a badger, looking awful, battling for his life. But he came to camp, vomiting, still taking his medicine while he was there, quite a remarkable young man. I saw him last week and his hair has grown back and he's looking pretty good. He's through it, the doctors and everybody think he's beaten cancer. And he told me a story. He lives in Wellington and he's a very capable motorcross rider. He's been round a dirt track at one of the local racing tracks for motorcross riders on an 80cc bike, not a big motor, and he's just done a time six seconds faster than anybody at any age and with any engine capacity has done around that track. Just this tiny little fellow, probably doesn't weigh 55kg, who I know that eleven months ago was fighting for his life. He's been one of our banner boys; he's fronted TV and poster work all while he was sick because he wanted to help us. He loves CanTeen and he wanted to help the organisation that helps. He has an enormous heart this fellow and epitomises Live Life.

There are three types of values – espoused (what people say they value), governing (the values that govern their behaviour), and desired values (the values that people want to have). The gap between governing and desired values is an opportunity for the organisation to grow. Some organisations also have a gap between the espoused and governing values which results in a belief that leaders don't walk the talk.

Those are my principles, and if you don't like them . . . well, I have others.

Groucho Marx

I did some work for a small executive team on values. After that session two of the four executives revised their CVs and left the organisation because they realised that there was a huge gap between the Managing Director's espoused and governing values that wasn't going to be bridged any time soon.

Values drive your decisions and are seen in your behaviour. So the best way to model a value is through your actions. People follow what you do, not what you say. The children's game 'Simon Says' is based on this principle. The way to help embed the desired values is to first act them and then tell stories about them. Tell these stories often. And if you live the values on a day-to-day basis, others in the organisation will help tell those stories for you.

When Sir John Anderson was CEO of National Bank the marketing team who had come up with a new strategy for increasing revenue approached him. Basically it was an increase in bank fees. According to the legend, Sir John looked at the proposal and then pointed to the values that were on a poster of the wall. He asked, 'Does this meet our value of looking after our customers?' Heads went down, feet were shuffled and 'no' came the response. 'Then I'm not signing off on this' and the proposal was scrapped. It spread through the organisation like wildfire that the boss at the top was living the organisation's values.

The key to telling a good values story is to know what that particular value means to you. Only then can you be clear about what you're communicating. For example, customer service means different things to different people. It may mean returning their call the same day to one person or getting back to them within a week to another.

Vero Insurance has a set of values and each value has an accompanying list of behaviours. These behaviours are divided into 'I Will' and 'I Will Not' lists. They are not prescriptive but rather guidelines that show what is acceptable behaviour in the organisation and what is not. It gives the staff a common language and benchmark that they can always come back to when having to make a decision.

Summary

» Be clear on what your own high-ranking values are and what they mean to you
» Align them to your day-to-day role at work
» Find examples where you lived the organisation's values professionally

Engagement stories

Engagement stories are stories that may share knowledge, coach a person, simplify complex ideas, break down barriers, communicate a brand, sell a product, or make a presentation more memorable.

Negative stories do have a place in organisational storytelling. They do not necessarily inspire people but they can be used to help learning and understanding. As human beings we learn through making mistakes. This starts as a toddler trying to learn to walk, as a child learning how to ride a bike, as an adolescent learning to drive a car. Then as an adult trying to figure out how to balance mental and physical well-being with a satisfying career while having healthy and fulfilling relationships.

So it's only natural that in order to learn we share knowledge, mainly by telling stories about what didn't work. An employee tells a co-worker, *'Barry did x and now Barry doesn't work here anymore. So don't do x, ok?'*

I have a friend who is the CIO of a major newspaper's online edition. I was discussing with him why the newspaper didn't put more positive stories in their paper. He told me that they track what stories are the top rating ones and the negative stories by far and away outrank the positive ones. This makes sense when you consider that when we hear negative stories our in-built survival system puts our attention on high alert as it may contain useful information to keep us alive. So it's a very small step to actively seek out lessons in the media. Or it could simply be a case of *Schadenfreude* – we experience pleasure from other people's misfortune and tragedy. This certainly explains why we laugh at TV shows showing funny home videos.

When coaching a person you're sharing knowledge, so these stories, although they may be negative sounding, will have a lesson and should paint a positive picture and set a goal for the person to move towards.

Because telling and listening to a story is a whole brain activity, storytelling is a great way to break down complex ideas and simplify communication. It can also break down barriers between people. The easiest way of achieving this is to get people together and have them share identity stories in a supportive environment.

Anyone in sales and marketing can tell you the importance of having a good story when it comes to building a brand and selling products and services. If customers connect to the story, then they will tell your brand story for you. In order for this to happen, you need to engage the customers' hearts and minds. It's beyond the scope of this book to look at storytelling within sales and marketing except to say – put all the latest sales and marketing jargon on the backburner and go back to basics – is your brand telling a good story?

When telling an engagement story the quickest way to connect with people is through humour. Emotions are contagious so if you use humour and are upbeat with a positive outlook and enjoying yourself, you'll attract others with a similar attitude. You'll find people will be more willing to help you and follow you as humour greases the wheels of relationships and communication. If you do a lot of presentations then humour is a must as it makes your message all the more memorable. The good news is that there are many different ways you can use humour in presentations.

I once saw two managing directors of separate competing companies both present to the managers of the two organisations about working together on a project. One was a storyteller who used jokes to create rapport, was very energetic and commanded the room. The other, whose presentation followed straight after, was by contrast more formal in his delivery but still managed to create a positive impression by using humour in his PowerPoint slides by using cartoons and funny images.

You may have a manager who isn't doing a good job of giving feedback to his team. Rather than just telling him to first praise what the staff are doing well before launching into what they're doing wrong, you may want to use an anecdote to help him remember this point. An example would be to point out that a barber lathers a man first before he shaves him. That creates an image in his mind that he will more readily remember rather than an abstract point about being positive first.

Summary
» Know what your desired outcome is and select the appropriate story
» Deliver the story in a genuine way
» Use humour where possible

Use CLEAR
What are the five rules of narrative?
The five rules of narrative are CLEAR:

C = Character undergoes change
L = Logical progression of events
E = Expectation circle
A = Association and reincorporation
R = Ride the curve

The above guide provides five CLEAR rules of narrative, and shows what characteristics and elements every *good* story must have. In order to achieve the desired effect stories have to connect with people. As we've seen, different objectives will determine different characteristics particular to that type of story but here is a general guide applicable to all stories.

I will show how the rules are applicable to more traditional storytelling, then relate that to organisational storytelling. Experience shows that referencing traditional stories helps people see the rules in action more clearly and facilitates the transference of the rules over to organisational storytelling.

Character undergoes change

It's paramount to understand that it's the *change* in the stories that people connect to. There is no journey without someone or something going through a transition. And helping people get through change is a fundamental requirement of all leaders.

Of course, as we've seen, different stories will have a different focus depending on the type of change required. Helping someone see that their attitude towards other team members is causing dysfunction will require a different type of story (engagement story) than helping a team feel inspired about reaching the new sales targets (call to action story). But no matter what the story, there has to be some kind of change. Let's compare telling a traditional story with organisational storytelling.

Traditional stories

In *Star Wars* Luke Skywalker starts off as a farm boy and ends up as a Jedi Knight. In *Lord of the Rings*, Frodo starts off as a happy hobbit and ends up saving Middle Earth. In *Pride and Prejudice*, Elizabeth Bennet despises Mr Darcy and yet by the end of the story there's no other man she'd rather marry. The heroes and heroines in these stories undergo change.

In the story you tell, the main character must change in some shape or form. Who is your main character? Is it you, the team, your customers or the organisation as a whole? Think also of the person or people you're telling the story to. What's the change you want them to undergo? Do you want them to be inspired about the new direction of the organisation and embrace change? Do you want a team to work more collaboratively? Do you want an individual to improve his or her performance? Whatever change you want will dictate what kind of story you use.

Organisation stories

Now the main character in your story doesn't necessarily have to be a person. It could be a subject like a product, a service, an idea or a process. Consider one IT technician telling another technician the story about fixing a recent system problem. In order to fix the problem the computer system had to undergo change. In this knowledge-sharing example, it is the computer system that is the main focus.

Logical progression of events

There must be a logical progression of events if the story is to help people make sense of your message. Stories generally move in a forward direction. Even flashbacks in stories help to drive the narrative forward. As stories advance, you can also extend them. Remember, extending is to flesh out the stories and give them colour. Think of advancing being like the skeleton of a body. It's what holds everything together as the action takes place. The extending is the flesh on the skeleton that gives detail to the overall picture. An example of advancing would be a story about a manager who was caught embezzling the company. Extending would be giving details of the manager, the amount of money and the embezzling method used.

Traditional stories

If you're watching a hospital drama on TV and all of a sudden an alien drops in through the roof, you disengage from the story as it's not logical and has violated the logical progression of the narrative. However, if you were watching *Star Wars* and an alien drops in through the roof, then it would be believable. This is because it's aligned with the next rule – the expectation circle.

Organisational stories

Is your story relevant and is it appropriate? Are you using a negative story to try to inspire people? Does your story have a point or is it self-indulgent? Do you need to get across just the basic information or do you have the time to flesh out the story more? It's not always practical or the right choice to give too much detail so take into account how much time you have, your audience and your purpose.

I worked with a company where senior managers were afraid to approach the CEO after 4pm because more often than not he'd launch into a story that would keep them there trapped in his office until well after 5pm. Sometimes a 'yes' or 'no' answer will suffice!

Expectation circle

The expectation circle is what we come to expect in any given communication. If you listen to a salesperson, you expect them to talk positively about their product. You expect a comedian to make jokes, you expect bankers to communicate more formally than mechanics, although both will have their own specific language and jargon. There is a part of our brain in our frontal lobes that is hardwired for expectation.

Traditional stories

Because our brain is a patterning device, we naturally create certain expectations. If you think of the Western genre you can automatically think of the types of characters you'd expect to find in such a story. You can effortlessly think of the locations where scenes would take place, objects, the kind of language used, even the common themes of Westerns. Images of cowboys, sheriffs, bandits, saloon madams, jailhouses, stagecoaches, cacti, tumbleweeds, quick draws, revenging the shooting of one's 'pappy' come easily to mind.

We expect these things in stories. However, this doesn't mean that the expectation circle is static – it can always be expanded. Until *Brokeback Mountain*, cowboys and homosexuality weren't automatic associations but they can be now.

Organisational stories

You need to be aware that before you tell a story you're always competing with another storyteller – the one that lives in your audience's head. They will have their own expectations, their own story and they will be listening to you to see if what you're saying fits in with what they're telling themselves. If it doesn't connect, then they will disregard what you're saying. We'll explore this concept of counter-stories in a later chapter.

Just as easily as people can create expectations from a general idea, they can create a story in their mind that tells them something isn't quite right. They may think that what you're proposing isn't going to work, or they begin to think you or the organisation's past performance isn't congruent with what's been communicated. They may even start thinking that what you're saying is threatening to their patch.

You can tell your story in a way that acknowledges what might be running through their minds and then lead their minds to an open place where they will at the very least consider what you're sharing with them. Storytelling won't work every time for everything but the more you consider the counter-stories that may be in the minds of your audience, the greater the chance of your story hitting the mark.

Association and reincorporation

There are two parts to this rule. Association is how the elements of the story connect with each other and reincorporation is the reinforcing of the main point, the change you wish to communicate.

Traditional stories

How do the characters in the story associate with each other, what's their relationship? How do all the characters, locations, objects tie in with the plot and advance the narrative? Having a meaningful change is more important than having lots of changes. In the fairytale *Goldilocks and the Three Bears*, there's only Goldilocks, three bears, their cottage and belongings and the woods.

Different elements, such as characters, themes and objects can be reincorporated. In *Goldilocks and the Three Bears*, the Three Bears are characters that start off in the story and then go for a walk in the forest. Goldilocks comes in, does her damage and then the Bears are reincorporated back into the story. Themes can be reincorporated or repeated. In the Goldilocks' story, the Papa Bear's porridge is 'too hot', the Mama Bear's porridge is 'too cold' and the Baby Bear's porridge is 'just right'. This theme is repeated for the chairs and ultimately the beds.

Objects can be reincorporated in a story. The James Bond stories give plenty of examples of this. James meets Q who gives him the latest gadget, for example, a watch that has a powerful laser beam. An hour later into the film James is captured by the bad guy – how does he get out? By using the laser beam watch that we were introduced to earlier of course. If he had just had the watch and used it and we hadn't seen it earlier, then we'd feel cheated by the story.

Comedians in stand-up comedy call reincorporation 'call backs'. The comedian Billy Connelly will tell one story and then 20 minutes later when telling another, he will reference something from the earlier story that gets a laugh of recognition.

Organisational stories
What's the connection, the relationship between your audience and your message? You don't need too many elements when it comes to having a good story. Have a few key messages that you repeat and reincorporate and that's it. Having superfluous detail clouds the clarity of your message. You need to reinforce your story. Rarely can you only tell your message once and be done with it. You need to walk your story around the organisation until the story takes on a life of its own and permeates the culture.

Ride the curve
Ride the curve means to be aware that storytelling is about taking the listener or reader on a journey. You can't start with the biggest bang or point of the story as it doesn't give you anywhere to go. This final rule cannot be utilised until the first four have been applied. The curve has its own logical progression of events and once you've started up the curve, you can't come back down. Coming back down makes your story anti-climactic and everyone will know where your story should have ended.

I was invited to participate in an international symposium on creativity. After two days of working together, I was instructed by the organiser to have the final say and close the symposium. I finished with a short dramatic piece that ended with a famous Maori saying. The energy in the room was electric and I thought, phew – nailed it. Then the organiser said that they just wanted to add a couple of things and you could feel the energy in the room drop as it became clear this wasn't the end after all and the magic was undone.

Traditional stories
In action stories, the big fight scene between the hero and villain happens at the end. In romance stories, the guy and girl get together at the end. In horror stories, the tension builds and builds. In comedies it gets funnier and funnier with the big pay-off at the end. In tragedy it gets sadder – in Shakespeare's *King Lear*, Cordelia dies at the end of the story. It would be anti-climactic if she died any earlier.

Organisational stories
You use story to shift people's mindsets so depending on the type of story, it needs to have a point and mean something to people. You may want to move them to action, to work more collaboratively or simply have them show up to work on time. So the story must build up to this meaning.

One final note on these five rules of narrative. Please remember, like all rules, these can be broken once you know them!

Use CLEAR to structure your presentations
The 5 CLEAR rules of narrative can be applied as a checklist when it comes to structuring a presentation. Use this checklist and you will always have an engaging presentation.

1. Character undergoes change
When putting a presentation together, ask yourself who the main character is. Is it your audience, your product, your key messages? Be clear on who or what you want to undergo change.

2. Logical progression of events
Ensure your presentation moves cohesively from one point to the next. Check that it flows and takes the audience along for the ride.

3. Expectation circle
You need to consider what the audience's expectations are. Do you want to meet their expectations or exceed them and give them something new? Are you speaking their language? Is your presentation full of jargon they might not understand?

4. Association and reincorporation

Make sure that your key messages tie in with each other. What can you do to link the key points together? For example, using a previous point to reinforce another or using a particular story? Where do you need to reincorporate your key messages?

5. Ride the curve

You need to think of your presentation as a journey. What journey are you taking your audience on? Remember, a presentation, like a story, has a beginning, a middle and an end. Think of the classic presenting wisdom:

a. Beginning – tell them what you're going to tell them
b. Middle – tell them
c. End – tell them what you've told them

When it comes to riding the curve, think of the ending you'd like your overall presentation to have. Is it a 'happily ever after' ending, a cliff-hanger, a grand finale, a choose-your-own-adventure, or a full circle story? You need to consider the way you will finish.

3: The When

The short answer

When leaders ask me when can they use storytelling, my usual reply is – 'When would you not use a story?' By now, you know its power and what it can do to improve communication so why wouldn't you use it all the time?

The key is you have to ask yourself how do you spend most of your time communicating and how could storytelling fit in? By asking how, you activate the reticular activating system – the part of your brain responsible for arousal and motivation. Have you ever bought a new car and then seen it everywhere on the road? That's that part of the brain at work. By asking yourself when could you use storytelling, your mind will open up and start looking for times when you can use stories.

Bear in mind that there are many different mediums of storytelling, whether it's books, movies, comics, television, newspapers, theatre, opera or the internet. The same applies to organisational storytelling. However, organisational storytelling works best when it's told verbally with face-to-face time between the teller and the listeners, whether it's one-to-one or one-to-ten million.

The long answer

I want you to think of organisational storytelling not just in terms of categories but rather as a whole concept.

You see, when it comes to storytelling there are no such categories as why, what, when, where and how. I use them because the Western mind thinks largely in categories. We like to break the whole down and put things into boxes to understand them. We perceive things in isolation as opposed to the more holistic way Easterners perceive. Our way of perceiving with a narrow, sharp focus lens is a hangover from Aristotle's box-thinking ways but storytelling can't really be broken down that way.

I'm now suggesting you start putting those categories together and think of the art and science of storytelling as a whole. Don't get me wrong, categories are useful to help us understand concepts but problems arise when we believe that the content we've put into the box can only stay there. It's like the fascination with personality profiling. Just as it's foolhardy to think that six billion people can fit into only one of 16 personality types, you do yourself a disservice if you think that you can only use these stories in the particular situations I'm about to disclose. There's no one right answer as to what kind of stories you can use in a particular circumstance.

So the best answer to the question of what story should I use when is: 'What does your instinct tell you?' Your years of hearing and sharing stories have created an unconscious, silent knowledge within you so that you will know when to speak up when asked. That's probably going to be a much more reliable guide than the techniques I'm about to share with you.

FIVE stories – when we tell them

» Giving a presentation
» Selling a service and/or a product
» Introducing yourself/company to a new client
» Inducting new staff
» Focusing a team on the goal
» Managing staff/client relationships – performance reviews, giving feedback
» Modeling behaviour, challenging unacceptable behaviour
» Influencing others, telling the boss they are wrong
» Shifting a paradigm to show a different way of thinking, enhancing creativity

» Delegating and teaching a new skill
» Engaging people, getting them to laugh, reducing stress
» Communicating within an organisation
» Walking the floor – sharing the vision, purpose and mission

In *Less is More* (2002), Jason Jennings studies the eight most productive companies of which The Warehouse is one. He recalls how he was standing in one of the Auckland stores speaking with a middle-aged employee working the floor who was able to talk about the company's culture just as eloquently as Stephen Tindall, the company's founder. The culture is an intrinsic part of a company therefore it lives in the minds and hearts of everyone who works there.

If you want to practise telling stories, then start in the privacy of your own home. Tell stories at dinner, at BBQs, on special occasions such as anniversaries and birthdays, and on Mother's Day and Father's Day. You can practise at farewell parties when people are going overseas or at reunions, at picnics and on family holidays. Basically create your own reasons to practise telling personal stories.

Dealing with counter-stories

I know that you believe you understand what you think I said,
but I'm not sure you realise that what you heard is not what I meant.

Robert McCloskey

In discussing the expectation circle, rule number three of the 5 CLEAR rules of narrative, I touched on how people have their own stories running through their heads. Don't worry, we all have this inner voice and we're all constantly talking to ourselves. And if you just asked yourself 'Do I talk to myself?' and it wasn't out loud, then that's the voice I'm talking about! It's a busy voice. We are able to think much faster than we can talk – about four to five times faster. While we can speak 120 to 150 words per minute, we can think at the rate of 600 to 800 words per minute.

For every story there can be a counter-story. As the old saying goes, 'there are always two sides to every story'. So while you're telling your story, people will have their own story in their minds. And the story people tell themselves is very powerful as it's their story and they retell it over and over in their mind. Now the downside is that there may be absolutely no basis for them to hold these beliefs. The 'narrative fallacy' is a term given to show how a story can trump facts even when it shouldn't. Because our brain thinks in narrative, it automatically ties facts together and makes interpretations of them.

You've probably heard that the Great Wall of China is so big it can be seen from the moon. This makes a great story but is totally false. Ah, but never let facts get in the way of a good story right? Imagine someone tells you about the time a particular brand of car they owned always broke down and then they shared the story of how they were late to their own wedding, and the bride-to-be thinking she was being left at the altar ran from the church in tears and couldn't go through with the marriage even after hearing the explanation.

Next time you were looking to buy a car and saw this brand, this story would pop into your head and you'd move on to another vehicle. The emotional power of this unfortunate person's story has more meaning to you than any statistical facts and information about the car's reliability for instance, you don't take into account the information about how he actually maintained the car in the first place – because that wasn't part of the story.

In the workplace a colleague may tell you that a particular client is difficult and as a result before you've even met this person you already have a preconceived story running through your head that the client will be trouble and will judge everything about the person from this perspective.

A Chinese folktale tells of a man whose axe went missing, and he suspected his neighbour's son. The boy walked like a thief, looked like a thief, and spoke like a thief. But the man found his axe while he was digging in the valley, and the next time he saw his neighbour's son, the boy walked, looked, and spoke like any other child.

Of course there can be a dark side to storytelling. It's a tool, just like a hammer is a tool. It can be used to create and destroy – it all depends on the intention of the person who is wielding it.

The story in peoples' minds may be in direct opposition to what you want. We all see reality differently and we see the reality we want to see. We are predisposed to suffer from 'belief perseverance'. This is when we tend to look for facts that support what we believe and ignore those that don't. This is summed up in the saying: 'People believe what they want to believe'.

If a group of people are suspicious about the head office of their organisation and think HQ doesn't know what it's doing they will dismiss the communication and believe that they, the employees, already know what's best.

Where there's a will, there's a won't

Ambrose Bierce

Michelle van Gaalen, Group Manager of Retail Banking for NZ Post, tells a story about dealing with people who have a strong counter-story.

I remember going to one store up North where the manager said to me 'Who do you want to talk to?' and I said I actually want to talk to those people in your team who are the most against the direction that we're taking. So she gave me a couple of people and we went out the back. I would have spent probably 45 minutes with them and they were completely against the fact that we were looking to measure our performance in terms of how much we've sold to customers. They were against the fact that we wanted to measure the experience our customers had, they were against a lot of the moves that we were taking to make sure that we could learn and grow around those elements. They were pretty hard and pretty direct which is great, I actually really enjoy that, and they just thought it was a whole lot of head office mumbo jumbo, and we were just doing it to make their jobs harder and to catch them out and the rest of it. So I just talked to them for 45 minutes and talked to them from a customer perspective, from an outsider perspective, and told them stories about how they would feel and what they would look for when they went into other organisations and what would a good experience

51

look like for them. And at the end of it one of them actually gave me a hug and said to me, 'I really understand why we do this now and I get it'. The manager rang me the week after and said, 'I don't know what you said but it's like you put a rocket under them, it's amazing'.

However, there is a positive antidote to this way of thinking and it's called 'cognitive dissonance'. Cognitive dissonance is what happens when the human mind tries to hold two opposing thoughts at the same time. It just can't. If you think you're not very good at public speaking but you have lessons and practise and you notice an improvement, and also get positive feedback from people then you have to change your mind and update your belief.

Now those people at NZ Post up North have a new story in their minds. Michelle van Gaalen told stories that gave the context and purpose of what the organisation was trying to do and painted a picture of the future for the employees. It's more than likely they are now champions of NZ Post's strategy.

People can look at the same event and see two totally different things taking place. It all comes down to perspective. The philosopher Bertrand Russell showed this with his famous line: 'I am strong-willed, you are stubborn, he is pig-headed'.

Annette Simmons in her book *The Story Factor* tells a story about a judge in the 1950s who was overseeing an argument about prohibition. When cornered by both sides on the question of alcohol he said: 'If when you say "whiskey" you mean the devil's brew . . . then certainly I am against it. But, if when you say "whiskey" you mean the oil of conversation . . .'. Here we see a wise man who can show both sides of the story without committing to either one.

There are no facts, only interpretations.

Friedrich Nietzsche

There are only two types of knowledge in the world: first-hand knowledge and second-hand knowledge. This first is gained through direct experience such as riding a bicycle. The second is gained through other people such as seeing someone else ride it or hearing how it's done. It's not always possible to give people the direct experience, so storytelling is the next best thing.

While people may look like they're listening to you, there is a difference between hearing and listening. Hearing is a physiological process where sound waves reach our brain via our ears and are turned into information. Listening is a psychological process of interpreting what you hear and turning it into information. If you think bombarding someone with facts, logic and rational analysis is the best way of getting them to listen and change their mind, then you'd be wrong.

So how do you deal with counter-stories when generally speaking, people don't want to change their mind? Only a diamond can cut a diamond, so the best you can do is to use a story that has the right message that opens the gates of their minds and lets them take on this new story as their own. This works because stories are less about facts and more about meaning. They can decide whether to let the meaning of your story in or not, but they'll be much more likely to open their minds to your idea if you give them the content in the form of a story rather than just the bare facts.

Stories	The facts
Leader	Manager
Engage hearts and minds	Speak to the head
Set vision	Plan
Align	Organise
Unlock wisdom	Get discounted easily
Are indirect and non-confrontational	Are direct and confrontational
Have life	Are inert
Inspire	Control

The story

In an old Jewish teaching story 'Truth', naked and cold, had been turned away from every door in the village. Her nakedness frightened the people. When 'Parable' found her she was huddled in a corner, shivering and hungry. Taking pity on her, Parable gathered her up and took her home. There, she dressed Truth in 'Story', warmed her and sent her out again. Clothed in Story, Truth knocked again at the villagers' doors and she was readily welcomed into the people's houses. They invited her to eat at their tables and warm herself by their fires.

Think of communication like crossing a street in a foreign country where they drive on the other side of the road.

1. You have to look in the other direction to the normal one first – i.e. look at what you want to communicate from the other person's perspective, rather than just from your own. Then look your way – say what it is from your perspective.
2. Then look back the other way – check that the person interpreted what you said the way you wanted them to.

If there is any one secret of success, it lies in the ability to get the other person's point of view and see things from that person's angle as well as from your own.

Henry Ford

Story is the best tool you have of getting into people's minds and hearts and as already mentioned, humour is the number one way of achieving this. Humour is a wonderful method of disarming hostility, whether it's overt hostility or below the surface.

I know of a manager in a financial organisation who had to deliver the news to his team that the brand rollout they'd been using and building up for the last two years was now scrapped and a whole different rollout was going to take place. He took a calculated risk and told them that there was not only new branding but a whole bunch of new processes plus a new computer system rollout. Everyone was up in arms for a moment before he shared that there were no new processes or computer rollout – just the branding. The team saw the funny side and no doubt there was genuine relief that it was only a re-branding exercise.

This doesn't mean that if you have to deliver bad news that you should be flippant – obviously you have to know your audience. But look for where story can be used. You may know another company that went through a similar experience and it worked out for them in the long run.

Maybe you have to deliver a data-heavy presentation with information overload. Before killing your audience with PowerPoint, bring story and humour to the party up front.

I saw a finance manager at Air New Zealand open his presentation with the line, 'Right, boring numbers time. If I haven't bored you to death by the end of this, then I'm not doing my job'. Everyone laughed and this relaxed the audience immediately as that's what they were all thinking. Knowing his audience weren't the financial types he had stayed away from traditional financial graphs and diagrams and instead tailored his data based on seats on a plane – something that everyone could understand.

With a little bit of imagination you can turn what may appear to be a challenging bit of information or a boring presentation into something engaging and thought-provoking.

When dealing with counter-stories that you can probably guess your audience is telling themselves, you need to address them. One organisation I did storytelling work for was about to undergo their seventh restructure in five years. The people were tired of living in fear, wondering if they had a job and the constant organisational change was unsettling. No amount of pointing out the facts on how this change was going to be good for the people would work. The leader had to deal with the emotions of his people.

Remember, we are emotional beings who rationalise. The leader had to be upfront and admit that the change was distressing, that they hadn't got it right in the past and acknowledge that everyone was sick of change. By doing this the leader was saying, 'I know what you're thinking', and once he had addressed this, the audience felt relieved, as if they had been heard and they could move on.

So the best way to deal with counter-stories is to be authentic, use humour if appropriate to point out the elephant in the room, and tell a story to open people's minds to see that there is another way of looking at things.

4: The Where

» Story starters
» Be a story listener
» Using other kinds of stories

Story starters

A man is always a teller of tales, he lives surrounded by his stories and the stories of others, he sees everything that happens to him through them, and he tries to live his own life as if he were telling a story.

Jean-Paul Satre

Your whole life is a library of stories. You simply need to make the time to sit down and reflect on your life experiences and you'll find the stories. In my sessions I often hear people tell me that they don't have any stories to draw on. What's more likely is that they are looking for epic stories in their life and therefore judge many appropriate stories as not being worthy. The more you sit and write down your personal stories, the more memories will come flooding back to you.

All we have in our life are our stories. Most people say that if their house was on fire and they only had time to save one thing, they'd grab their photo albums – a physical collection of their memories and the stories of their life.

The following are some starters to help you flex your memory and storytelling muscle.

Find a quiet place, close your eyes and take a deep breath. When you breathe out, feel any tension leave your body. Count down from five to one and allow yourself to become more relaxed as you count down. In this relaxed state, allow your mind to ponder some of the following questions. Have a pad and pen close by so you can write down your memories.

1. Reflect on your professional career
   » What work experiences have you enjoyed the most and why?
   » What work experiences have you least enjoyed and why?
   » What mistakes have you made on the job?
   » What lessons did those mistakes teach you?
   » Who has helped you in your career?
   » What did they do that stood out for you?
   » What have been the major turning points in your life and why?
   » When are you at your best at work and why?

2. Reflect on people in your life
   » Which teachers had a positive impact on you?
   » Who were your childhood heroes and why?
   » Which relative's house did you enjoy going to and why?
   » What do you like about your closest friends?
   » Any flatmates who stand out for you? Why?
   » Which bosses have you admired? Why?
   » What kind of celebrity would you like to be?
   » Anyone you've been scared of?
   » What lessons have you learnt from past relationships?
   » Whose friendship and company do you enjoy and why?
   » Who is your best friend at work?

3. Reflect on events in your life
   » Any memorable birthdays?
   » A time when you overcame great odds?
   » What are some of your proudest achievements? Why?
   » What events have made you sad? Why?
   » What make and model was your first car? What did you like or dislike about it?
   » A family vacation that stands out?
   » A time when you were romantic?
   » When did you take a big risk and it paid off?

» What were some of your most embarrassing moments?
» What's your earliest childhood memory?
» What sports or hobbies interest you and why?
4. Reflect on your values
Think of which core behaviours are important to you and you'll have your values. Think of a time when you personally lived your organisation's values. The following are some starting points.
» When in your life have you experienced or shown kindness?
» When has trust been important to you?
» What key values did your parents teach you and how?
» When have you felt guilty about something you've done or said? What value of yours did you violate?
» Think of a time someone has angered you, what value did they violate?
» When have you been creative?

When you've written some memories down, the next step is to look for what the story tells you or reveals about you. You will have stories that you can use as identity stories, value stories and engagement stories. There will be stories that you can use to teach others, coach behaviour, build rapport and become an overall more effective communicator.

There will be success stories and stories of missed opportunities. Some of our most negative experiences in life teach us the most. By turning these painful life experiences into stories we create meaning in our lives and they help shape who we are and how we continue to live.

I worked with the young leaders of CanTeen, an organisation of teenagers living with cancer. One of the more senior leaders who was only 20 years old said to the leaders in training that getting cancer was the best thing that had ever happened to him. It gave him the kick in the butt that he needed to focus on the direction of his life and enjoy every moment.

Be a story listener

To speak is to sow; to listen is to reap.

Another way to gather your stories is to listen. A good storyteller is a good story listener. When you listen to other people's stories, it will spark stories in your own mind. Your brain thinks in association so when someone shares a time when they averted near disaster, your mind jumps to a time when you almost skied into a tree. You can't help thinking in association, because your brain is a pattern machine. You can use this to your advantage. When you hear someone telling a story, whether it's them sharing what they did on the weekend over a coffee or a speaker at a conference, pay attention to what images pop up in your mind. What personal story of yours does it remind you of? Where and when could you use this story?

The most important question anyone can ask is: What myth am I living?

Carl Jung

I worked with an insurance salesman helping him craft an identity story. He said he couldn't think of anything so I asked him to share a positive experience he had had recently. He said that a few weeks ago he went diving with his seventeen-year-old son. He thought that as his son got older he wouldn't want to hang out with his dad so thought it would be good if they had an activity they could do together. He enjoyed diving and his son showed an interest in it so he put him through dive school. On their first trip the son didn't want to go out diving, he wanted to stay in bed and then laze around the beach. The father insisted because he knew if he didn't they would never go. They went diving and the father shot off looking for crayfish to catch. He looked around for his son who was taking his time and really taking in the amazing underwater world. It taught the father to see the beauty of the sea with fresh eyes, to take the time to appreciate the wonders around him. It was a shared experience that brought him and his son closer together.

This story indirectly shows a number of things about the teller. He knew there would come a time when his son would want to do his own thing so he had to have the foresight to plan ahead. It also showed him that we often don't appreciate the things we do have and don't know their true value. Do I need to point out the link between this learning and the whole concept of selling insurance? This was a personal story he could share with people to illustrate the positives of planning ahead.

By actively looking to collect stories that you can use, you will soon find yourself with a strong database of stories that you can draw upon for the appropriate occasion.

Using other kinds of stories

This book is focused on organisational storytelling and using vision and values stories, stories to show who you are and stories to engage hearts as well as minds.

You can also use generic stories as engagement stories. These stories can be metaphors, analogies, proverbs, fables, folktales, myths and legends, fairytales, parables, historical stories, even some jokes can be used as appropriate stories. I'll just touch on some of these and share how they can be used.

A common device is to use an analogy. An analogy is a simple way of getting your message across. It's when you transfer information from one concept (e.g. your current project) to another concept (e.g. an onion). You may talk about the many different layers of the project, how much of the development happens out of sight and that when it's time to use the results of the project, hopefully it'll bring tears to your eyes.

You can use this by looking for areas in your presentation that are especially heavily fact-based or figure-orientated information and decide what the message is. You do this by asking yourself 'Why am I sharing this information'? Then ask yourself 'What can I compare this information to?' Ensure your comparison is accurate, test it on somebody and see if it makes sense to them. A health professional may say something like 'smoking kills three million people a year. That's 20 loaded jumbo jets daily. It's hard to picture three million people but we all know what a jumbo jet looks like'.

Analogy is more effective when the audience has experience of it. This is why sport and military analogies are often used, usually too much! And be careful of your analogy. Sport and military analogies are about competition. If it's collaboration you're after then they're not appropriate.

Many people have experience of gardening or at least know of it so you may compare your team to a garden. This team we're building is like working on a garden. We need to pay attention to the occasional weeding and getting rid of things that aren't working. More importantly we need to focus our effort on what's growing successfully and make sure we keep nurturing the team as a whole.

Using a story is a great way to provide an answer to a complicated question. I get asked by people who want to be an excellent communicator how long it takes to develop these skills. Because there's no one right answer I sometimes tell the following story to make a point.

A young but earnest Zen student approached his teacher, and asked the Zen Master: 'If I work very hard and diligently how long will it take for me to find Zen?'

The Master thought about this and then replied, '10 years.'

The student then said, 'But what if I work very, very hard and really apply myself to learn fast. How long then?'

The Master replied, 'Well, 20 years.'

'But, if I really, really work at it. How long then?' asked the student.

'30 years', replied the Master.

'But, I do not understand,' said the disappointed student.

'Each time I say I will work harder, you say it will take me longer. Why do you say that?'

The Master replied, 'When you have one eye on the goal, you only have one eye on the path.'

You can use stories as examples of creative thinking and finding solutions to problems. I use the following story to show people the benefits of lateral thinking and asking better questions.

A farmer had a neighbour whose dogs were coming on to his farm and killing his sheep. Rather than using lawsuits, barbed wire and a shotgun to solve this problem, he asked himself a question. Instead of asking 'How can I stop my neighbour's dogs from killing my sheep?' he asked himself, 'How can I get my neighbour to help me protect my sheep?' His solution was to give his neighbour's children lambs as pets. The neighbours then voluntarily tied up their dogs and the families became friends.

Storytelling is at the heart of every culture and folktales express this cultural history and reflect our humanity. You could use a folktale to make your point, encourage certain behaviours, break down silos and barriers between business units and show it's important that we treat others with respect. The Grimm Brothers' folktale about the old man and his grandson does exactly that.

An old man whose eyes had become dim, ears dull of hearing, and a body that could no longer move without shaking would sometimes spill his soup and let it run down his mouth when he sat down to eat. This disgusted his son and his son's wife so much that they made the grandfather sit in a corner facing away from the dinner table and gave him a poor earthenware bowl to eat out of. Once his trembling hands could not hold the bowl and he dropped it, shattering it on the ground. He was scolded and from then on rarely given enough to eat. He would look at the table from where he sat with tears in his eyes but would say nothing.

One day his grandson, only 5 years old, was collecting bits of wood and holding them together with bits of thin rope. When asked by his father what he was doing he replied, 'I'm making a little trough.' When asked what for, the little child responded, 'For Mummy and Daddy to eat out of when I am big.'

The parents looked at each other and began to cry. They brought the old grandfather from the corner to the table and always let him eat with them, never saying a word if he spilled his soup.

I know of a senior manager of a company who had to make a presentation to a relatively hostile audience. He successfully broke the ice by acknowledging that sometimes management got it wrong and shared the following joke.

A man in a hot air balloon realized he was lost. He reduced altitude and spotted a woman below. He descended a bit more and shouted, 'Excuse me, can you help me? I promised a friend I would meet him an hour ago, but I don't know where I am.'

The woman below replied, 'You are in a hot air balloon hovering approximately 30 feet above the ground. You are between 40 and 41 degrees north latitude and between 59 and 60 degrees west longitude.'

'You must be an engineer,' said the balloonist.

'I am,' replied the woman, 'How did you know?'

'Well,' answered the balloonist, 'everything you told me is, technically correct, but I have no idea what to make of your information, and the fact is I am still lost. Frankly, you've not been much help so far.'

The woman below responded, 'You must be in management.'

'I am,' replied the balloonist, 'but how did you know?'

'Well,' said the woman, 'you don't know where you are or where you are going. You have risen to where you are due to a large quantity of hot air. You made a promise, which you have no idea how to keep, and you expect people beneath you to solve your problems. The fact is you are in exactly the same position you were in before we met, but now, somehow, it's my fault.'

This is just a taste of how you can use other stories as a leadership tool. If you want more stories I have listed some of my favourite books in the Recommended Reading section.

5: The How

» Preparing your story
» Telling your story

I'm keeping this section of the book focused more on the telling of a story rather than providing a guide to presenting. There are plenty of good books on how to improve your presentation skills and I've listed a couple of my favourites in the Recommended Reading section. However, the tips for improving your storytelling are relevant to improving your overall presenting skills as well.

Organisational storytelling is very much an oral art form. I've broken it down into two parts: the preparing of your story and the telling of your story. Each of these parts consists of two specific areas, so there are four areas in total. Obviously the scale of these different areas will differ according to your situation. You probably don't need to start a one-on-one coaching session standing on the table, gesturing wildly with a grandiose 'Friends, Romans, countrymen, lend me your ears', just as you wouldn't make eye contact with only one person when talking to a hundred people in an auditorium. However it's only the scale that changes, all four areas apply no matter the story.

When it comes to you putting all these parts together and telling your story – don't try all the parts at once. Choose one and focus on developing that area before moving on to the next. Becoming a better communicator doesn't happen with a swish of a wand – it takes time and practice.

Preparing your story

There are two components to putting your story together:

1. Structure
2. Mindset

Structure

Be on purpose

When you know your purpose, you'll know which story to use. Do you want to inspire an individual, team, department, or the entire organisation? Do you want to get buy-in for an idea, sell a product, or simply entertain your audience? Knowing your purpose will tell you whether you should use a positive or negative story, how long it should be and what its key point needs to be.

Use CLEAR

Use the 5 CLEAR rules of narrative to check that your story has a point, is relevant, engaging, takes the audience on a journey and that the main character, whoever (or whatever) you decide that may be, undergoes change. If you use these five rules of narrative then you will have a beginning, a middle and an end – everything a good story needs.

Be short and specific

As a general rule, your stories should be relatively short and always illustrate a specific point.

Mind your language

Words influence an emotional response from people. There have been studies that show when people are primed with words such as 'slow' and 'old' they actually walk more slowly and take more time to get to places. So since you have to use words to communicate, choose the best ones.

> *Words are, of course, the most powerful drug used by mankind.*
>
> Rudyard Kipling

In most cases you'll want to put across a positive message, so you need to take care creating a positive mental image for your audience. Eliminate the negative by framing what you're saying in the positive.

The brain thinks in pictures and the word 'not' is abstract so it can't visualise it. In order to process the concept of 'not', the brain has to create an image of exactly the opposite. It would be like me telling you right now *not* to think of an icecream . . . and then asking, 'What flavour was it'? The word 'not' can hide in such words as don't, can't, won't, doesn't, shouldn't and mustn't.

The simple strategy for positive framing is to tell people what you want them to think about, not what you don't want. Or as I've done just here – use both!

Framing is used in advertising, which is all around us. Going back to our imaginary ice cream, which would you prefer to eat, the 80% fat free one or the one with 20% fat?

I use framing at the start of my sessions. If I tell people about my background in improvised comedy and that we'll be doing improv games throughout the session, they'll feel a sudden rush of fear of looking foolish in front of their peers. So I have to carefully frame how I use improv exercises in my sessions. I avoid the word 'games' and share how the art of improvisation is a wonderful vehicle for experiential learning as it helps people gain personal insight. The exercises engage people on a physical, intellectual and emotional level and act like a mirror enabling them to see themselves more clearly. People are then more relaxed and have fun while they're learning. This gets a very different response than if I was to start with, 'Okay, game time, everyone up!'

Frame the story

On a larger scale, you also need to put an overall frame to your story. This gives your story purpose and helps your audience to get the meaning you're after. A painting can look very different according to the frame that surrounds it. It is the same is with a story. You want to ensure that you and your audience are 'on the same page'. If you don't put a frame around the story then they may miss your desired meaning. Don't leave it to chance – make sure the context of your story is understood.

Often people fear looking foolish in an organisation and the fear of being judged and criticised by others is often what holds people back in being themselves, the key to being a great communicator. I explain how fear is the biggest killer of creativity and personal growth. With that frame, I then tell the story about a psychologist who went into a school and asked the five-year-olds, 'Hands up who is an artist?' All the kids put up their hands and said with great enthusiasm, 'Me, me, I am'. He went to the next year group up and asked the six-year-olds the same question. Fewer kids put up their hands and there was less enthusiasm. By the time he got to the 11- and 12-year-olds, only two kids put up their hands. And they didn't do it with any enthusiasm but slowly with sideways glances to see how their peers were judging them.

Every child is an artist. The problem is how to remain an artist once he grows up.
Pablo Picasso

Use humour

Humour is the number one way to connect with and engage an audience. This doesn't mean you have to be a joke teller or stand-up comedian but it does mean you have to try to be humorous. If you feel you don't have a very refined sense of humour then you're going to have to fake it till you make it!

Of course, if you're doing a serious presentation then perhaps humour may be inappropriate. However even the most tense occasions require a break. That's often why you'll find laughter at funerals and humour in tragedies.

When President Ronald Reagan was shot in an attempted assassination and taken to hospital he is reported to have said to his doctors, 'Please assure me you are all Republicans.' If he can say that in those circumstances then you can definitely find some humour in what you're doing.

The best humour comes from your own experience. Insert humour into the story you want to tell or find a funny personal story where there's also learning that has taken place. Humour isn't a 'nice-to-have' when you're communicating – it's a 'must-have'! And remember if you are going to make fun of anyone and get laughter at their expense, the safest person to make fun of is yourself!

Use novelty

The brain is attracted to novelty, as it will be forced to make sense of it and find a pattern. If there's a way to enhance your story then use it. If you have a special skill, for example you can do impressions, walk on your hands or play the kazoo then it may be appropriate to look to incorporate and reincorporate this talent into your message.

Know your audience

If you're talking to a group of people in the organisation other than your normal team or to a group outside the organisation then it pays to find out as much as you can about them. This will assist you in knowing how best to communicate with them, how much jargon you can use, how to tailor your message and whether to use humour to ensure you achieve your desired outcome.

When good stories go bad

You're human. Things are going to go wrong at some point so accept that now. You'll lose your way, forget something important, get sidetracked and so on. It's a good idea when doing a presentation to have a couple of prepared strategies that you can call upon when needed. Have a glass of water off to the side that you can walk over to and have a drink. That walk will buy you precious seconds so you can gather your thoughts and get yourself back on track.

If you lose your way you could also try asking the audience, 'Now where was I?' If they don't know, you can quip, 'So you weren't paying attention either'. If they do know, let them know that they just passed your test to see if they were listening.

Murphy's Law is alive and well. Things will go wrong during the telling of a story or a presentation that have absolutely nothing to do with you. Some of them you can be prepared for (and you'll look like a star!), some of them you can't be. The more prepared you are in knowing your content, the more confidence you'll have in dealing with those curve balls.

A person I was coaching tells of the time he had to do a big presentation at an Australasian travel conference. His Australian counterpart did a very high-tech presentation. Then it was his turn. As he took the stage he could hear his introductory music get slower and slower until it died completely. He saw the look of panic on the face of his assistant as she stood next to the technician shaking her head at him signalling that they'd lost everything. He took a deep breath and just started talking to the audience. His PowerPoint slides with all the numbers and information were gone so he told the audience stories relevant to his presentation. It freed him up and he got his message across in a way he wouldn't have dared to attempt otherwise. He felt it was the best thing that could have happened to him. He had people coming up to him afterwards telling him it was the best presentation of the conference.

Remember: when things go wrong it's an opportunity for humour! And if you are good-natured about your mistakes, your audience will love you even more.

My most memorable entrance has to be the time when I was about to walk into the training room carrying all my equipment and materials for the session. In full view of all the participants who I would be spending the day with, I walked straight into one of the clear sliding glass doors. Hard. You can't ignore that. You have to call it. I told them 'Now that goes down as my greatest entrance ever', which got me more laughter. Funnily enough, one of the participants in the room had broken the doors a week earlier when they were wooden thinking that they were swinging doors so I used that as a bond between me and that person. I then went on to use what happened as an example of what we're not going to do – barge down doors but rather use effective communication to open doors instead.

Mindset
Have a strong intention
One of the rules of the mind is often whatever the mind tends to expect,

tends to be realised. The mind thinks in images and the unconscious mind will always try to follow that image in your mind. So set a positive intention every time you have to give a presentation, have a sales meeting or any time you need to be an effective communicator.

Know your purpose and consciously think of your intention. Your intention may be that you're going to actively listen to the client, really connect with your audience or simply have a good time at the front of the room.

If you think you can or think you can't, you're right.

Henry Ford

They're on your side

The audience wants you to do well as a communicator. They certainly don't want you to bore them when you communicate with them – they're on your side.

At the very start of my acting career I felt nervous going for auditions because I felt judged by the casting directors, after all, that was their job! However, I later did an acting workshop run by casting directors where they shared that they always wanted people auditioning to do well. They saw their job as getting the best audition out of the actors. That came as a surprise but a very welcome one. It totally changed my perspective. Within a week of hearing that I nailed my first major audition and got the role.

Anchors away!

All information is received through our senses. Your five main senses are visual (things you see), auditory (things you hear), kinaesthetic (things you touch), olfactory (things you smell) and gustatory (things you taste). Your visual and auditory sense can also be triggered by internal stimuli as well; namely the things you see in your mind and the voice/s you hear in your head.

Anchors are sensory stimuli that trigger a certain response. It may be a thought, or an emotional or behavioural response. Whenever you hear a particular song on the radio it takes you back to a certain memory (audio anchor). Whenever you see the shoddy work done on your house by a tradesman it triggers a specific emotional response (visual anchor). When you walk past a café you smell the coffee beans roasting and you pop in to grab a coffee (olfactory anchor). The smell of coffee triggers that behavioural response.

Knowing this, you can set yourself up to use anchors to get you into a positive state to communicate with people. You may be nervous and need to relax your energy. You may be tired or flustered and need to raise or re-direct your energy. The following are suggestions that people in my sessions have said they use. It is by no means a complete list. There are crossovers because anchors are personal. For example, classical music can raise one person's energy, while it can relax another. The key is to experiment with different stimuli so you can find which anchors work best for you. Try them so you make an informed rather than a preconceived decision and keep what works and discard what doesn't. You may very well be surprised about what puts you in a great mental state.

Sense	Raise your energy	Relax your energy
Visual (internal)	visualisation, running through the presentation	visualisation
Visual (external)	pictures of inspirational people, images of your goal	pictures of loved ones, scenes of nature
Auditory (internal)	positive self-talk, affirmations	self-hypnosis, mantras
Auditory (external)	music, motivational speakers	music, chimes, listening to comedy
Kinaesthetic	exercise, yoga, dance	mowing lawns, hot bath, walking, breathing exercises
Olfactory	after shave, perfume, oils	smell of nature, oils, flowers
Gustatory	coffee, alcohol, chocolate, energy drinks	alcohol, herbal teas

My improvised comedy troupe, The Improv Bandits, warm up for every show with a particular kinaesthetic exercise that forces us to connect with each other while simultaneously raising our energy. This is so we hit the stage energised and ready to go. We have done this for over 13 years so when we do it, we know that it's show time and all the hassles and stress of the day melt away as our minds and bodies focus on the job at hand.

Be the special you

People will tell you to be yourself and that's true but when presenting you have to be the 'special you'. When you go to the theatre, read a book or watch a movie, the people holding your attention aren't just normal people doing normal things with nothing interesting happening in their lives. There would be no story! Likewise, when you're communicating to someone and wanting to convince them, influence them, inspire them – you can't just be the normal you.

I worked with a senior executive in a major financial institution. Before we started our session I had secretly hit the record button on the video camera. He was talking to his staff who were there as the trial audience about his weekend. He was animated and his voice was alive. I told him we were ready to start and he immediately became a presentation robot. His voice went flat, his arms dropped to the side as if he dare not move again throughout his presentation. Fortunately we had this transition captured on camera and he could see that he was able to connect and communicate as a human being in a corporate setting.

Be vulnerable

For this senior executive it was a question of not wanting to be vulnerable. Usually, the higher people go in an organisation, the more fear they have. It may be a fear of being caught out and looking like they don't have all the answers or a fear of losing their position and the flow-on social and financial effects that may bring. It sounds counter-intuitive but vulnerability for a leader is a strength. The more you are able to reveal yourself, the more people connect with you. They see your humanity, they feel connected to you.

A branch manager of a bank I worked with took this on board. She had scored poorly on a 360° feedback survey from her staff. She didn't know what to do. I suggested that she sit down with her staff and tell them exactly that and ask if they had any suggestions. At first she was horrified as she thought that as the leader she should be leading the way. I pointed out that if she didn't have any followers then she wasn't really a leader. She sat down with her team and almost moved to tears, told them that she didn't know what to do to improve the morale of the team and wanted their help. They warmed to her immediately – they saw her humanity. The next 360° feedback results were through the roof – in her favour.

Telling your story

The two areas of importance for telling your story are:
1. Voice
2. Physicality

Voice

Be the storytelling you

Generally speaking, your story should be delivered in a normal conversational tone. Of course you can add drama and flair to the story when appropriate but on the whole you'll be delivering stories in your natural voice. If your natural voice is a monotone, then you'll definitely want to get some voice coaching.

Mastering the paralanguage

Paralanguage is the vocal elements of speech – the volume, tempo, tone of voice and pitch. You want to be able to vary these elements as it gives you control of your audience. Trust me, they want to feel safe, which means they want you in control. You may want to suddenly raise the volume of your voice to shock your audience or gradually lower your voice to draw everyone in.

The actor Edward James Olmos, who played the police chief in the 1980's TV show *Miami Vice*, discovered that when in character, if he spoke very quietly, everyone, the cast and crew included, would be quiet so as to hear what he was saying. He found that it gave him high status. He also didn't look at Sonny Crockett, the character played by Don Johnson, when he talked to him for eight episodes, which he found also raised his status.

Increasing the volume generally means more energy is generated. Be aware that your voice always sounds louder to you than everyone else. Unless you're wearing headphones – then you're probably shouting.

You can vary the tempo with which you speak. In one study it was found that between those who spoke quickly and those who spoke slowly, the quicker speakers are thought to be experts in their subject. And remember, people think much faster than you can talk so if you're speaking too slowly, they'll be way ahead of you, or asleep. However, slowing down the pace periodically can add impact.

One way to vary the tempo is to use a powerful pacing of words or 'Trilogies'. Trilogies are lists that contain three items. Famous ones include 'I came, I saw, I conquered' and 'the Father, the Son, and the Holy Ghost' and Benjamin Disraeli's 'Lies, damned lies and statistics'. Look to craft your own trilogies as they are an excellent way of grabbing attention or even finishing off a story. George W Bush finished his address to the nation on September 11 2001 after the Twin Towers attack with 'Thank you. Good night. And God bless America'.

Your tone, the sound quality of your voice is very important. People will respond to your tone at an unconscious level and it carries meaning.

A schoolteacher friend of mine once used an angry tone to two of his students when handing back their work 'This is some of the best work you've done. I'm very proud of you'. Their faces fell, they dropped their heads and after a couple of moments looked up confused as they realised what he'd said.

Your vocal pitch is where your voice registers – high or low or somewhere in between. Breathing and vocal exercises can help extend your range although it's largely determined by the tension of the vocal chords. Varying the tone and pitch may be useful if you're adding dialogue and characters to your story.

Use the power of silence
You've heard the saying, 'It's not what you say but how you say it'. Sometimes it can be what you don't say. Pauses and silence can draw in an audience, it can give them time to reflect on what you're saying. The power of silence can be used to emphasize a point, to enhance humour, get attention or convey seriousness. Silences always seem longer to the person speaking but you have to allow time for people to process what you're saying. Remember, the difference between hearing and listening is understanding.

Ask not what your country can do for you . . . ask what you can do for your country.
John F Kennedy

The only thing we have to fear is . . . fear itself.

Franklin D Roosevelt

The name is Bond . . . James Bond.

Ian Fleming

Keep it fresh

When you tell a story it should be alive. This means you might tell it in a slightly different way each time. This is fine. You're not reading from a page (you better not be!), and speaking is different to reading. You can take your time, you don't have to be word perfect and you can search for words if you're genuinely in the moment. You can add dialogue to the story, take on a character, move around as all this helps bring the story to life and make it memorable.

Say it again

One way to emphasise a point is to repeat it. One way to emphasise a point is to repeat it. So what I'm saying is, if you really want to emphasise a point, repeat it.

In the Maori language, if it's important – it's repeated. You are welcomed with: 'Tena koutou, tena koutou, tena koutou katoa'.

And one of my favourite Maori proverbs:

He aha te mea nui o te ao?
(What is the most important thing?)

He Tangata, he tangata, he tangata.
(It's people, people, people)

Using repetition is powerful. You can repeat the same line at the beginning to start a different point the way Martin Luther King used repetition in his 1963 speech, 'I have a dream' and the way John F Kennedy did in his inaugural address in 1961– 'Let both sides explore . . . let both sides, for the first time, formulate . . . let both sides seek . . . let both sides unite . . .'.

Show, don't tell
An actor's job is to show the audience if they're angry, ecstatic, in love or homicidal – not to tell you these things. The same principle applies to you as a storyteller. You have much more impact when you show something rather than explain it to the audience. If you're telling a story that involves a seagull giving you some good luck by hitting you with its droppings from up high then you don't need to tell the audience how you felt. A simple look up at the imaginary seagull with whatever expression you had says it all.

Have it, don't show it
Another actor's maxim. You don't even have to show the emotion – you just have to have it. You don't have to act being angry, like shaking your fist at the said seagull and stomping up and down. That's a caricature of anger, not characterisation. Just have the emotion in you and it will show automatically.

You may think that you're not an actor but make no mistake, a great communicator is exactly that. I hope you're not reading this book to be a good communicator. The world is full of those – aim higher! If you're a leader then you need to be a storyteller, a performer. This doesn't mean you're fake. You have to be authentic. Charisma is no replacement for authenticity. But you have to get your message across. Unfortunately someone who epitomises this is Adolf Hitler. He didn't rally a nation with pleading 'come on guys, let's do it'. He mixed passion (no matter how warped) with performance and it moved people.

All the world's a stage, and all the men and women merely players.
William Shakespeare

You don't have to ooze charisma but obviously it can help you get your message across. Charisma usually comes as a result of people being effective leaders, not the other way round.

Brent Impey; CEO of MediaWorks New Zealand, tells of the time he saw Nelson Mandela speak in person. 'I never really believed in the concept of charisma until I went to a dinner party in Wellington one night and he was a guest. You hear that stuff about the hairs standing up on the back of your neck, but they actually did. Everyone else I knew there had the same experience. I've never felt it since and I've seen Bill Clinton. He was supposed to be the same but he's not a patch on Nelson Mandela.'

Enthuse!
Be enthusiastic about what you're talking about as it makes you more engaging, whether you're talking about a financial forecast or the team achieving a goal. The word enthusiasm is derived from the Greek words *en theos* meaning 'the god within'. So you need to have energy! If you're not passionate about the topic, look for something in it that you could be genuinely excited about or interested in. You owe it to your listeners to be enthusiastic. Again, if you are, you will show it in your voice, body and attitude.

Have sense appeal
You know from the section on anchors that we take information in through our senses and that when we remember something all the different parts of our brain work together to re-create the memory. So if you want to be influential, and want people to remember what you say then appeal to

people's senses. Think to yourself, 'How can I get all the audience's senses firing?'

Non-verbal communication
The first time
It's important to note that people are sizing you up before you've even opened your mouth. You are always 'on'. You need to pay attention to how you appear – what you're wearing, your facial expression and how you're carrying yourself.

Smile
When it comes to non-verbal behaviour, it's your face and eyes that most people look to for information. So be genuine, be positive and most importantly, tell your face about it. We are only open to be influenced by people we like. If your audience doesn't respond to you, despite your story making rational sense, their emotional brain will go 'nope', and they will discount everything you say. And then their rational brain will kick in and they will find 'logical' reasons as to why they ignore your message.

This sounds obvious. Smiling and other non-verbal behaviours are very important. Moving towards others, sharing a gaze whether it's eye contact or both looking at the same thing and imitation are all driven by instinct to help build rapport.

Connect then communicate
Making eye contact with your audience is a must. There are three key reasons:
1. Authenticity – Westerners especially trust people who make eye contact when speaking to them
2. Connection – your audience feels connected to you when you make eye contact
3. Feedback – you can monitor your audience and see how engaged they are by making eye contact

Don't be put off if you find the audience is quiet and looking away when you're telling a story. It doesn't necessarily mean that they're not listening. The nature of storytelling means people go into themselves as they personalise the story and this may give the appearance of looking disinterested. Obviously if they're snoring then you need to rework your story!

Be congruent

We as human beings cannot not communicate (love those double negatives!). We believe body language over words every time! If you've ever had the experience of asking a loved one what's wrong and they say, 'Nothing' as they pull away from you, the little alarm bell in your head should start ringing. It's important that your body language is congruent with what you're saying.

There are three main uses of body language:
1. To replace speech – e.g. nodding your head to indicate 'Yes'
2. To reinforce speech – e.g. giving a thumbs up while saying you're good
3. To display (or betray) mood – e.g. rolling your eyes when someone says something you don't believe

The separation of psychology from the premises of biology is plainly artificial because the human psyche lives in indissoluble union with biology. The mind and body are one.
Carl Jung

Communication is a whole-brain activity where the words we use are coordinated with physical gestures.

In an improv comedy performance, I had an audience member sit in front of me. I asked her to put her hands behind her back and I put my hands through her arms so that my arms became hers. My fellow performer interviewed her and we had been told in advance that she was very lively and would be a great person to interview. However she gave us nothing but monosyllabic answers and made us work very hard to make the interview entertaining. After the performance I joked with the organiser that we had been set up. We looked over to where the person we interviewed was standing and she was chatting away in a very lively manner. I noticed that she was using her hands a lot while talking and realised when we took her hands away for the interview, we lessened her ability to talk.

Mind/body presence

Although it's your body that shows whether you have presence or not, presence all starts in the mind. The way to have presence is to have a mind that is detached. Detached from the fear of failure, detached from trying to be good, detached from judging your self-worth as to how successfully you communicate. When you have that detachment, you are left with an inner confidence.

Like the millionaire in the Hawaiian shirt, you're not trying to ram your status down anyone's throat by proving yourself. You can't try to have presence. It's called the law of reverse effort. The more you try to do something, the further away you get from it. If you try to have presence then you'll invest too much ego into it and this just lowers your status.

While having presence is about being comfortable with who you are, there are certain things you can do to enhance your physical presence. Stillness is very powerful and when you move, you move with purpose. Being calm and breathing deeply gives the appearance that you are in control.

Remember: It takes time and practice to become an excellent communicator. Practice and perfect these storytelling techniques and you will become a person of influence, an inspiration to others and someone who gets things done. This will make you a valuable leader in any organisation.

Presentation checklist

The following is a handy checklist I run through before I do a presentation or training session. It just ensures that I have most of my bases covered.

Mindset

» Why is it me that is speaking and what are the expectations?
» What anchors will get me in the right mindset?

Audience

» Who am I presenting to?
» How many people am I presenting to?
» What is their level of comprehension of the subject?

Content

» What am I presenting about?
» What are my key messages?
» How am I going to hook their attention at the start?
» What stories can I use and where?
» What images/video clips/other resources can I use and where?
» How can I keep their attention?
» How do I want to finish?

Structure

» How long do I have?
» How and where can I edit the content so I can finish ahead of time?
» How can I use the CLEAR structure?
» Where do I need state changes?
» If a Q and A session is required where do I position it?

Delivery

» What is the appropriate pace and tone for delivery?
» Where can I use the power of silence?
» What areas of content require certain vocal emphasis?
» What tools will I use e.g. Flipcharts, PowerPoint, none at all?

Venue

» Where am I presenting?
» What do I know about the venue?
» What are the technical arrangements? (microphone, lighting, etc)

Practice

» Who can I practise on?
» Should I read aloud to myself?
» Does my presentation finish before my allotted time?

Part II
Stories in Action: The Interviews

Interview with Bob Harvey
Mayor of Waitakere City, Auckland

Bob Harvey became Mayor of Waitakere City in 1992 and has served six consecutive terms at the time of writing. He has been awarded the Prix UNESCO Villes pour la paix in Stockholm for services to peace and won the United Nations-backed personal lifetime achievement LivCom Award in 2008. Waitakere City also won a LivCom Award for being the most 'liveable' city in the world. He is one of only a few mayors around the globe to be honoured as a Global Mayor for Peace and the Environment.

WJ: What role does storytelling play in your life?
BH: I'm not only a Mayor, I'm a historian, I'm a keeper of the stories, the tales, the history, the legends of the West [Waitakere City is west of Auckland]. When I was about 15 I noticed people started telling me stories and I would be absolutely fascinated by them. I believe that to tell a story is to become a story yourself. You become the story you are telling and our life is a richness of stories and other people's lives. So I consider myself created by the stories that I have been told. We are like a blank canvas. When I was a young man, I was a sponge and I sucked up stories. I couldn't get enough

stories of people's lives, good and bad. My grandparents told me stories, ghost stories, life stories, and they just told them and then it was up to me to make sense of them.

WJ: In your role as Mayor, how do you set a vision for the city?
BH: When I came to Waitakere, I was very committed to create a story for the people here. That story was a great story, an environmental story, a sustainable story, and I told that story like a storyteller. I treated this city like a script because I knew of no other way of doing it. I knew no way to be the Mayor other than to write a massive, epic film called 'Waitakere'. And I would be the director, and I would be nothing else. I would simply say here is the script and you must not move from your script. The script would be called an 'Eco City'. It will be green, it will be fantastic and we will treat each other well and we will try and banish from this city, a bit like Camelot, bad and terrible things. We will love our children, we will work for the land, we will work to keep the forests of the Waitakeres, and we will build a city to be proud of. A good story has got to have a feel for the listener. You can't tell a story without captivating people and you can't tell a story without believing in that story yourself.

I have kept to the script and every year, in January, I review the script. And it is now in the closing phase. In October 2010, with the creation of the Super City, the movie will be shown. Having a vision for the city and telling it as a story is the only way I can deal with this business. It's the only way I could deal with it without being talked out of it or having my mind changed by people. It consistently keeps me on track year after year after year rather than just taking advice from the last person I met. If it isn't in the script, I'm sorry we ain't going to shoot that scene.

Now I tell the story of Waitakere internationally. I've told that story in Istanbul, London, Washington, Japan, China, and people bring me to their cities to tell the story of how we created one of the world's finest environmental cities. We've achieved this great story together. As the director, I had to find a great cast. I had terrific people, people who shared common visions. Some people I had to teach how to act but that wasn't too much trouble. I just gave them a job and say I am inspired by you. I didn't check on them very much. As long as they knew the story and were in character, they would be a terrific environmentalist. They would get volunteers, they would be people who thought the community had so much to offer and they would become advocates. And all I did as director was to shoot the scenes, by asking 'How's it going?' or saying 'Let's do this'. And some people didn't like me very much but I'm sure the people who act in movies don't always like the director, but they like the story.

WJ: How do your past stories feature in your leadership?
BH: When I tell people a story about what I want them to do, I talk about the past. I tell them what used to be and how bad it was. It's important to understand why people did those things, and why we should not let those things be repeated. If you don't understand the past, you will never be able to interpret the future. I admire Councillor Corban, former Mayor and probably my fiercest rival for this job for the last 17 years. Councillor Corban will always stop a meeting and tell a story about the past. Others may think 'here we go again', but I encourage it as he has a story to tell. He might say 'When I was a boy, Henderson railway station had one train every 10 hours, now we've got a train every 10 minutes' and it will lead from commenting how bad that was, to how good it is now and finally to the question, 'Can we make it better?' So I like to keep the past alive and on the boil with stories that are anchored and glued together by a sense of history and place. Stories need to have rules and certain elements and they must own those two things. We're talking about ancestors and we are talking about now.

WJ: How do you inspire your people to fulfil the vision for Waitakere?
BH: I have always got a story to tell. I tell them at environmental meetings to remind them of the great story we're creating. I tell them in art meetings to inspire them to build art galleries and libraries for us to own our heritage. I tell stories about extraordinary people from the West. People like Maurice Shadbolt, the author who lived in this city and worked here. People like the biologists Lucy Cranwell, who was one of the world's great biologists and found many trees in Waitakere, plants, and bushes, that had not been discovered. I tell my stories by revealing the potential that was here so that people here understand that they just didn't happen. They didn't fall out of the sky; their heritage has been built. I share the message that we have to reach our potential by realising that we have been given this unique opportunity to shine. So let's not be less, let's be more.

Interview with Steve Bayliss
General Manager of Marketing, Air New Zealand

During the tenure of Steve Bayliss at Air New Zealand, the airline went from the aftermath of near bankruptcy to becoming the 'Best Airline in the World' – as judged by *Air Transport World*. Air New Zealand has embraced storytelling as a method of creating a positive culture change with great results. It's marketing group has also become the most awarded in New Zealand, picking up numerous domestic and international awards for design, loyalty programs, creativity and communications. Prior to joining Air New Zealand, Steve worked at companies such as Lion Nathan and Coca Cola. He is a regular speaker and adviser to a variety of organisations on marketing and branded cultural change.

WJ: How did Air New Zealand come to be a storytelling organisation?
SB: We didn't originally set out to be a storytelling organisation but we quickly found that storytelling was the only way to get our message to our people and this was the relatively simple imperative. It began from a notion of trying to work out our message as we went from that period of brand vandalism, through to the early 2000s. It was about rebuilding the brand through to the last four years and rebuilding the culture of the business. Thinking about how we went about that journey, I think two things kicked it off and they both suit using storytelling. One was determining what we valued, and the second was how we were going to do it.

I personally cannot stand this notion of vision, mission and values in companies, nor the idea that you have two separate guides, one for the organisation and one for the customer. How you treat your people and how you treat your customers will be one and the same. Fortunately our CEO, Rob Fyfe, supported this viewpoint. To spend all that time on vision, mission and values is a complete waste of time and is useless to employees. I often joke that in every company's value statement are the classics, 'honesty, respect and integrity' and they have just got to have them. How many of your employees wake up in the morning and think 'Today I'm going to come to work and I'm going to lie, treat people poorly and then steal some stuff'? In the instance that you have someone like this working for you, what's the likelihood as they leave the office in the afternoon with the stolen laptop, they'll see the value statement on the wall and they think, 'Bugger, I'd better put this back'?

So why would we spend time on it? I love the Ritz Carlton where they have one thing that they asked people to think about to be an employee, which was their mantra, 'Ladies and gentlemen serving ladies and gentlemen'. And you go, 'This is delightful'. It's simple. If you're an employee you know exactly how you're meant to behave – as a lady or a gentleman. You know how you're meant to treat people. We wanted to get away from all of that business of fluff language and find out what is it we wanted to stand for.

We're a very New Zealand company, and we looked at four attributes about what it means to be in Air New Zealand and to be a New Zealander. And they were 'Welcome as a Friend', 'Share your New Zealand', 'Can-do' and 'Be Yourself'. These four attributes are the *how* you go about the tasks that you need to in completing your job. It's also the most important and valuable aspect of how people experience the Air New Zealand brand. In the airline category the human factors of the business are far more valuable than any seat, any lounge, any advertisement that we produce. Not only is it the most important expression of our brand, but also the most important driver of either loyalty or affection to the brand. If we disappoint someone, we can't bring them back with an advertisement. So that's part one for us, cleaning out the clichéd corporate language and giving people a really simple framework for being with Air New Zealand.

The second bit, the 'How we're going to do it', was as important. I reflected on Air New Zealand and where it was at with our evolution of customer service and thought, 'We've got a problem'. As organisations grow you go through a period where the customer service is random. You have a bunch of people who are effectively self-directed and self-motivated and doing their best. Some of them are really good, some are okay and some are terrible. Most companies go through the notion where you want a predictable outcome and certainty about what's going to happen with the customers. That's when you get the customer service training module and the rulebooks.

Air New Zealand was classic with this because we're a very rules-driven industry. We defy gravity at hundreds of miles an hour so we need rules. There's a big difference between the rules that exist for the safety of our staff and our customers and commercial rules. The notion in the past of how you get certainty around customer outcome is to try and make it predictable, which means you have a lot of manuals and training programmes to outline what to do in different scenarios. Two things happen. One fails really quickly to adapt so you end up making a lot of mistakes because the situations are so fluid and so random. The second one is that every time something comes up that you haven't experienced before, you need a new rule. So the rulebook becomes heavier and heavier to the point that they become worthless.

I think that the next evolution is about saying 'How do you get consistent quality of customer outcome that isn't determined by rules, that's determined by some guidelines that people have and their ability to use their judgement'? I think the only way to achieve that is through storytelling. When we wrote it up originally we wrote it as an old graph, a really simple two-dimensional graph. At one level customer service can be very scripted and exact and that's trying to make it predictable with a lot of rulebooks. At the other end of the continuum it can be very spontaneous and adaptable. On another continuum it could be delivered as a formal servant or as a relaxed friend. For example, Singapore Airlines would probably operate as a formal servant. But at Air New Zealand we couldn't culturally do that. As New Zealanders, as a group of people, we treat people as a mate. The person I'm serving today could be my new neighbour tomorrow. We're not good at just sticking to the rules, we're better at spontaneity and adapting to circumstance. By thinking about achieving a consistent quality of outcome within the context of the fact that we're New Zealanders, we think within this notion of 'Be a friend', thinking for yourself, and can-do. You then need to think about how you can bring all that to life and you end up realising you can't write a training programme for that and you wouldn't want to.

WJ: How do you balance the necessary rules and regulations of your industry with allowing people to be themselves?

SB: There are two sets of rules at Air New Zealand. Those that exist for the safety of our customers, our employees and our assets and they're sacrosanct. Then there are all the other rules. None of those rules are more important than common sense, judgement and fairness and so we need to talk about that. After you free people's imagination you can engage them in what it means to be an Air New Zealander, about being a friend, being yourself, and being a New Zealander. The only way you can bring that to life for people is through storytelling. By doing that, you say that 'Yes we'll have some commercial rules to guide our decisions'. However that will only get you the predictable, not consistently excellent because being consistent fails every time something unexpected comes up. We've used storytelling as a critical element to helping people on the journey to work out what welcoming people as a friend means for them.

There are two important elements about storytelling, and it can be where some companies go wrong. The first bit is that you need to let people work it out for themselves. If you take a new experience, some people are quite good at handling it and others are awful. We spend a lot of time helping people work out what it is to be an Air New Zealander in their own frame of reference. I can tell a lot of stories about how people have used being a friend as an attribute to help them, and I try to tell quite a broad range of stories. Sooner or later one of them will 'ping' with a person and they think that will help me. Whether they're an introvert or an extrovert, whatever their style is. So they can adopt that attribute in terms of how they work at a personal level. We invite people a lot and by telling enough stories sooner or later one will ping.

The second element, and I think it's critical, about storytelling is that you need to give people an arrow to point at otherwise stories become this worthless, random set of twaddle as opposed to telling the stories about how someone has behaved or treated somebody. You've got to have the right point of view. For us it's living our four attributes – can-do attitude, be yourself, be a friend, and share with New Zealand. These give an important frame of reference in terms of setting a target.

WJ: How do you use stories to hit these targets?

SB: We bring these four attributes to life through everything we do. There's our CEO's weekly message, which tells stories every week. There will be a theme that he wants to talk about, for example how he's feeling about the tourism industry, the job summit, or something that he's involved in. Every week he integrates a story and every one of those stories will trace back to what it means to be an Air New Zealander.

Every single member of the executive team uses storytelling in every presentation they do. You just won't find any of us present a bunch of overheads and fact-based charts. We may use them but every time we do we'll pepper it with storytelling. Every leadership conference we do is all about storytelling. We will use different people to bring to life their experiences, what it is to be an Air New Zealander through storytelling. We are always pointing back at the target and never losing sight of that. You probably need a couple of evangelical zealots, which I guess is part of the role that I play in the business. Whether it's talking to one person or a hundred, internally or externally, day after day we are talking about our journey and telling stories about it. It could be through informal gatherings, or through quite structured core-training type programmes in customer service.

WJ: You have people who champion storytelling and help filter the concept down from the executive team. What did it take for them to get others to buy into using storytelling? Were there naysayers and how did you deal with them?

SB: I don't think there were any naysayers. This is probably because there was such strong advocacy for the direction we were taking from our CEO. We didn't start this journey gently. We called the top 150 people together and started telling stories from ground zero and people very quickly saw the power and the impact. This started to filter very quickly through the business and you could see storytelling in all parts of the business.

Our four attitudes come through from how we screen and induct people, right through all the training programmes. Some recruits are easier than others and quick to come on board. Clearly very customer-facing roles get it very quickly. You spend a lot more time talking about how you want everyone to treat each other. Internal culture and the way you treat your customers are indivisible. For a group like baggage handlers it can be as much about how we want to treat each other, and demonstrate to our peers and colleagues the notion of working with a friend. If someone new joins the team there's the 'can-do' and 'be yourself' which is the ability to have a bit of fun. We don't need to be serious all day. We'll do a lot of things at work and socially around that. So for them it's a lot more about culture, but they may take a bit longer to join in on the journey. For other parts of the business it's easy and they can do it really quickly.

WJ: How do middle managers or team leaders use storytelling?
SB: I think it varies depending on a few things. What you find is people emulate communication styles that they find to be effective. By effective I mean the combination of gaining something valuable and being entertained. Nobody likes sitting through an hour-long presentation and being bored senseless. The reality is that if you think every time you stand up to present that you're not in the entertainment business, you're a nutbag and are sorely mistaken. You may think you're communicating valuable information but if you're not entertaining about that journey then you're not communicating.

Middle managers and team leaders will also use storytelling in their training programmes. The reality is that most of them think that storytelling is effective after seeing it done and they think 'I'm going to have a crack at that'. They'll probably start by telling the same stories that they have heard told. Then they relay the information that they got to their teams. I've seen an awful lot of managers evolve to clearly building their own little mental database of stories that they want to whip out to amplify points.

WJ: Is there a story database? Do you collect stories?
SB: Yes we do collect stories. We have an active database and we solicit those stories through directly asking for feedback and they just filter into various email inboxes, or running promotions. Saying everyone who gives us a story about how you demonstrated 'can-do' at Christmas for example will get a Huffer T-shirt, whether the story's good or bad. We keep a database of that. I think probably every individual keeps their own mental database. I have a book all handwritten which is just my favourite stories. They're stories about customer service or welcome a friend, be yourself, can-do. That's my personal database and the stories that resonate with me and I know I can tell well. I'll often go through my own database before a presentation and

think for that piece of information I want to impart, I'll use that story. It's very simple now. I think as well as the company story database, your personal database is a very valuable thing. Some of my stories will be very short and some will be three or four pages long.

WJ: Can you give me an example of a story that relates to your business goals?
SB: We talk a lot about being yourself, which to me is the hardest of our four attitudes for people to get their heads around. Air New Zealand's had three or four reasonably good years. There was pretty strong public support and I think there's some genuine danger in that. If you start to become a bit successful, big, corporate and bureaucratic, that starts to sound like a few companies in New Zealand we don't like much. You can't bond with big, corporate and institutionalised, you bond with human beings. By allowing people to show a bit of themselves in a fun, fresh and human way this is important in maintaining Air New Zealand's connection.

We have some guys in Tauranga at the regional airport who recently had part of their PA machine break so they had no 'bing-bong' for announcements. They were wondering what to do. They decided to have a staff competition and everyone had to have a turn to see who could do the best 'bing-bong'. You can imagine the stories from it, they've probably been amplified but that doesn't matter. Everyone did it differently. On reflection of that you go, what's the first thing you would have said if you worked for Air New Zealand on that day in Tauranga? You'd probably say, 'You wouldn't believe what we did!' The first thing you'd think if you were a customer at the airport that day is, 'Hey I was in Tauranga, you wouldn't believe what they were up to'. It's very humanising. How could you think of Air New Zealand at that moment as being institutionalised like the other big companies? What a fun sense of humour and all they did was just have a bit of fun on the day. But we're able to say to others here's an example of being yourself and why it is important to us as a brand. You're again looking at the moral of the story, which is absolutely critical.

WJ: How did the story get back to you?
SB: I was doing a training programme on our attributes and generally when I do that I tell a couple of stories at least about each of the attributes and what

they mean. My 'be yourself' stories must have been rubbish because this guy who worked at Tauranga airport stuck his hand up and said, 'I think this is a great example of be yourself, so he told the story'. So I stole it off him.

WJ: That's a great story in itself! Someone says 'I can beat your story!' and now you've taken it and you're sharing it.
SB: A lot of where the stories come from happens like that. The stories start to circulate and they probably build and take on a bit of a life of their own as they move around. They probably get a bit richer and a bit more colourful but that's okay. The four attitudes provide the relevance. Nobody really uses storytelling for reasons other than that. Having that home to point to has been so critical in the change in our culture and service ethic.

WJ: How do you develop storytelling skills in your people?
SB: We have programmes for people who are interested in being better storytellers at our leadership colleges. We have several a year that we put a couple of thousand people through. That often picks them out, in terms of those who want to develop those skills. Then there's a lot of people who just pick it up from observation. We've seen people who have become very good storytellers. On the rare occasion, you see people who you know are never going to be that comfortable with it and that's okay. If it's not something you're good at then don't force it, it will sound terrible. That's part of being yourself. You might bring someone else into the meeting to help strengthen that talk for you.

There are a number of really good storytellers throughout the business who constantly use stories to reinforce key messages, always tracing back to the goals. People have got different levels of skill at expressing themselves. Stories are generally mundane or only interesting at the start. It's learning how to tell them in a way that amplifies them very strongly. A little bit of theatre and creative licence adds value. Plus I think the secret to helping people tell good stories is to tell the story from an organisational perspective. When that's done, it's like giving them the moral of the story. With the moral of the story given, it's just a matter of making the facts fit into it.

WJ: How else did storytelling play a part in the change management process?

SB: It played a huge part in determining what we wanted to be, giving ourselves a target and engaging people passionately in that purpose. Stories bring the target to life, and keep it alive. Your stories need to evolve, grow, change and get richer with time. But I don't think that even for a moment you should get bored with your journey. You should never think, it's okay we can relax and take our foot off the gas, the change is going well, how about we focus on something else for a little bit? I think the moment you have any one of those conversations you're in trouble, because your people aren't bored, they're quite engaged and entertained. There's no point getting your people talking about things they can't affect like the global financial crisis for example. It's much better for them to focus on how they can affect the quality of the outcome for our customers and employees.

WJ: What's the next step for Air New Zealand?

SB: The way we talk about and introduced the Air New Zealand journey to people was through an invitation. We invite you to join our journey, to accompany Air New Zealand. The four attributes are put on board to work out what they mean to you. We didn't force people or penalise people who weren't ready for that journey yet. That means individually we have some people who are phenomenal and some people who aren't all the way there yet. I think the next evolution for us in bringing it to life is moving from individual responsibility to collective responsibility.

It's almost like a family structure. Families are quite demanding on each other, we hold each other to quite high standards in terms of the rules of the family, in terms of behaviour and values such as morality and all of those types of things. When someone steps outside we tell them very quickly. There's nothing worse than that, 'You've let the family down', type of thing. We've all heard that from our mothers and that made us feel worse than any punishment. I think our next evolution is bridging that transition to individual accountability and family accountability. I think we'll use storytelling to make that journey come to life.

Interview with Dick Hubbard

Founder of Hubbard's Foods
and former Mayor of Auckland

Dick Hubbard set up his own food company in 1988 and has been a champion of promoting social responsibility in business. He founded the New Zealand Businesses for Social Responsibility (now the Sustainable Business Network), and was also Mayor of Auckland from 2004 to 2007. 'Clipboard' is a printed newsletter filled with inspirational stories, quotes and ideas that goes into every box of Hubbard's Foods.

WJ: How have you used storytelling in your career?
DH: I like to use storytelling in speeches that I give and with the work I do at Hubbard's Foods. We are just doing an exercise now that has been in the making for 21 years. We're capturing company and staff stories in a little booklet form that we make available to the staff and will use only really for internal purposes. We did it 11 years ago so this is round two. We have got some wonderful stories amongst the staff. Some of them, a lot of them, never, ever get back to me but they're very, very important at the time that they're captured. We're doing it to capture the wealth of stories, give a historical perspective, what has happened, how it has happened, give a human face to the company and hopefully there will be lessons to be learned in what has happened and how it's happened. So the stories won't necessarily all be inspirational ones, there will be stories of failures and stories of things that didn't go right and stories of when the wheels came off.

WJ: What is important about leaders using storytelling?

DH: I've found that stories are very powerful ways of getting the message across and if you just scribble the theory and you don't give stories to illustrate, you're actually losing the impact quite significantly because a story changes the theory to practice.

I also believe stories have to be woven into the message and stories by themselves don't cut the mustard. This is a point I make very strongly. Inspirational stories by themselves don't actually mean anything. They're almost sort of pop psychology, they might give you a quick buzz for half an hour or an hour after you read them but they don't change your thought patterns just by themselves and in isolation, you need more than that, you need something behind them.

For me, there are three categories of stories. There are stories of what's happened to you, there are stories of what's happened to other people, and then there are parables, which never actually happened to anybody. Sometimes its appropriate to have a parable, or you could pick up a story about something that has happened to somebody else, which you've heard or read about, and sometimes it's personal about what's happened to you. As Mayor I used to go along and do a presentation at the induction programme that was held about every two months for new employees. I would tell the parable about the bricklayer building the cathedral as opposed to the other bricklayer who was cutting the same stones but only to make a dollar.

WJ: Do you have any stories of your own that you use?

DH: Yes very much so and I think the ones that have the most impact are the things that have happened to me. One story I used to give in the mayoralty to an appropriate audience, was that about 18 months into the role I got invited one day to become an honorary member of the Auckland Rotary Club. So one Monday I trotted down to the Auckland Rotary Club and I had a lovely lunch at the Auckland Club. I sat next to six very interesting businessmen and talked about all sorts of things, you know the where are you going on your skiing holidays, where do you travel overseas, what's the best new car, what's the best suburb, all sorts of things that you talk about at that sort of place. They had a very good guest speaker who talked about protecting intellectual capital and then had a lovely lunch. It finished at 2pm on the dot and just by serendipity, I had been invited down to the Auckland City

Mission for that afternoon. Between 3.00–3.30pm they put on a late lunch, which is the meal of the day for homeless people. So at 3.30pm I'm having an afternoon lunch with a group of six homeless people. Exactly the same number at the Rotary lunch but instead of a table with the white tablecloth and nice cutlery and crockery, there was a chipped Formica table, plastic knife, plastic fork and a mug of orange juice. Instead of talking about what skiing holidays we went on, we talked about life in the streets. Instead of what suburb we lived in, it was talk about which is the best bridge to sleep under. It was just contrast, contrast, contrast right through. It had an amazing impact on me that you realise that there are two sides and how easy it is to respond to the pressures and concerns of the privileged but how the people who are homeless are real people as well who also have needs and wants. Just because they don't vote or don't dress nicely doesn't mean we have to ignore them.

WJ: Where would you use that story?
DH: At the right time. I would use that story if I were talking at a Rotary Club or a church group or something like that. Somewhere you can use the story to be reflective. You pick a story for the venue. I like to have about six or seven or eight core stories and I pick the right story for the occasion, circumstance and audience. There's nothing worse than having the right story for the wrong audience. I also have different versions. I can complete the story in two minutes or ten minutes, depending on the time available and the types of points that I'm trying to make.

WJ: Do you have a story that reveals you to your audience?
DH: There is one story I tell that is a little straight to the point about what you feel is appropriate to you as a behaviour, is not always seen as appropriate by somebody else. And the illustration I give is when I was up in the Islands, we used to go snorkelling along the reef in the lovely clear water. I had a friend who had a boat and one day he said you know we're snorkelling along the reef so I'll throw a line over the stern, hang onto the line and I'll go slowly and you'll see a lot more than swimming along the reef. So I did this and was hanging on. He was going probably about two or three knots and we were working our way up along the reef. Suddenly I realised that yeah this was fun and dandy, but how would a shark see this situation? A bit of meat

being trawled behind a boat, I may as well have had a fishhook on my belly, a shark's perception of the situation was totally different to my perception. So beware of the sharks, they see things differently. When I realised that I got out of the water very, very smartly.

I also have a deeply personal story that I share. It goes back about 25 years ago when I was with a previous company before I started my own company. I went along to a half-day seminar on negotiating tactics. I loved it. It was psychology negotiating, how to get the best deal, to get win/win situations, how you psychologically out-manoeuvre your opponent, to find out their strengths and weaknesses, how far you can go, how to set them up, etc. There's a lot of psychology to negotiating; you want to try and have your opponent ending up feeling as if they have won something as well. Obviously the thing about negotiating techniques is to get as much as you possibly can out of the situation. So I thought that was great and I went back over all the techniques and about two or three weeks later we had a property to purchase for the company I worked for. I used the techniques and I got a really good deal. Instead of paying $500,000 I paid $498,576 or something, you know, right down to the last dollar. I analysed the people we were buying it from, I found out their strengths and weaknesses from the textbook, and I got a good deal.

And then about two months later, just before Christmas, I decided I would buy my son a pushbike so I looked up Trade and Exchange and there was a $70 bike for sale in Mt Roskill. So I rang and talked briefly over the phone, and the negotiating techniques came into play. I tried to find out her circumstances and whether I should do a deal or not. I fronted up to her house in Mt Roskill, a state house, with peeling paint and I thought, okay here is someone who is fairly desperate for cash. So I went in and assessed her situation standing there. She had snotty-nosed little kids standing beside her, so I thought she's pretty desperate for cash, I can do a pretty good deal here. Part of the negotiating techniques is that in those sorts of situations you always take the cash out of your pocket and wave it in front of someone's nose. So I took out $50 dollars and waved it in front of her nose; she looked at me and you could see the cogs turning over and I told her I thought the bike was only worth $50. She agreed. So I gave her the money and as I turned round to walk out she just said two words, 'You bastard'.

And I had those words echoing in my ears for a long time. When I gave that bike to my son for Christmas, I had a hollow feeling. Instead of the joy of giving him the bike, I thought of the woman who I deprived of $20 and how her kids may have been deprived. And what I realised then was how important it is not to take your business techniques and to impose them on your personal life. I was taking what I was doing in the business world, and a business set of values and imposing it on my personal life. And I realise it should actually be the other way around, what we should be doing is taking personal values and imposing them in business. Ultimately, business is people. The problem is if you have one set of values for business and one set of values for your private life, the two will merge and you can't actually put them in separate columns. You can't be a Jekyll and Hyde – a family Jekyll and a business Hyde. If you're rough and tough in the business, either you or your employees, it will be reflected in your family values and your family life. One of the greatest contributions business can make to society is to actually make sure the right set of values is in place.

That is a story about one of those moments that changed my life. I think all of us in our lives have moments like that, just something you box up. I was totally, totally, totally wrong here. Those two words, 'you bastard' just spoken softly as I left the door.

WJ: When do you use this story?
DH: I have often used it to business audiences. When I've got to give a speech to any audience, I get a bit of an assessment of who the audience is, what time of the day it is, etc. The sort of story that's relevant to a breakfast meeting is quite different to a meeting that is after dinner where they want something a little bit lighter. Stories have to be adapted or selected according to the circumstances. The story always has a right place, right time and a right audience. I also think people like stories that are personal or slightly self-deprecating. There's nothing like laughing at yourself with somebody in order to earn their trust. If you tell that shark story you can usually get a good laugh out of it. The 'you bastard' one is not a story that you'd expect the audience to laugh a lot at.

WJ: Are there any other ways you use stories as a teaching tool?
DH: We've found that our 'Clipboard' stories have been very powerful as people tend to read it over breakfast, which I think is always a good time.

We do a million-copy print run at a time, which is every six weeks so we say somewhat jokingly that we're the biggest circulation of any written material in New Zealand. We've had some quite amazing reactions from some of the stories that we've told. There was one woman who wrote to us about when she had been snorkelling up the Coromandel peninsular in the summer holidays. She'd dived down about six or seven feet and got her foot caught in a rock. She started to panic and almost drowned. By the time they got her to the surface she was unconscious and they only just saved her. They had to rush her off to hospital, put her in intensive care, and when she came out of all of that she really struggled. She became very depressed and suicidal. And one day she said she read my 'Clipboard' newsletters and it just snapped her out of it like that. That was a reaction to a very specific problem she had at that point in time. So one story at that point in time is just enough to flick somebody, which I think is quite different from me hearing a story and saying okay can I improve myself as a result of hearing the story. It wasn't in isolation either as the whole theme of that 'Clipboard' was appropriate for her.

WJ: How do you use stories when working with the management team at Hubbard's Foods?

DH: I illustrate the points I'm making when I work with the management team with a little story or an anecdote. It makes it more personal and makes it more relevant. It depends what group I'm talking to. I was talking to the people that were doing the development work so I gave them a story about how I made my first rice bubble. We put in a plant to make rice bubbles and this was about 10 years ago. It was very difficult because there was no literature on it and we had a whole lot of machinery and most of it didn't work. We made tons and tons of rice pudding before we got anywhere, horrible, gluggy stuff that didn't pop up. We were going for about six months and we had about a 100 tonnes of rice pudding. One day I was looking through the results of the trial in a bin. I was running my hands through and suddenly in the palm of my hand was a perfectly formed rice bubble. I still remember the moment and I felt like shouting 'Eureka' – I realised we had made one. There was something there we had done right to this grain of rice, and all we had to do was find out what it was and make sure every grain of rice got the same treatment and we were there. I didn't quite run down the street naked like Archimedes but I still remember to this day that feeling of looking there and seeing one rice bubble. The rice just cascaded through my fingers, a bit like a miner's pan where you've got tons and tons of silt going through then suddenly the muddy water goes and you've got a golden nugget in the bottom of the pan, it was like that sort of sensation. The moral of that story was 'Keep going, keep going, keep going, and don't give up'.

Interview with Cath Lomax
Head of Sales and Service, ANZ

Cath Lomax has had various roles within ANZ and is currently a part of the Retail Team. ANZ Retail Banking has been using a cultural program called 'WOW' to deliver stories since 2005. In 2007 they won an Auckland Human Resources Institute of NZ award for their WOW program and it has been a major part of raising staff engagement.

WJ: How did WOW come about?
CL: WOW was created with the idea around ensuring a customer has a good experience, a WOW experience. It was also about how we WOW each other and progress the cultural program. We did a lot of work with partners and all the executives got together and talked about it. We asked the question, 'How can we get something out there?' and came up with WOW.

WJ: How important has storytelling been to the WOW program?
CL: There have always been changes in the banking industry but none more so than in the past few years. Through that whole time WOW has been our constant vehicle. It is the cultural program of the ANZ retail business and that's been a very important, stable focus for our people and for the business. That's something that's not going to go away. We have staff that have been around for 30 years and have seen so many initiatives tried and they can't believe that a program based on storytelling is still going. And it's not going to stop.

When it was first launched it was quickly recognised that one way that we were going to be able to get WOW going would be to start telling stories. Getting people to tell stories about how a customer has had a WOW customer experience. We set up a whole structure where staff or branch managers or leaders would send in WOW stories. It was a slow start as the first kind of stories we got were like 'we smiled at the customer and they were wowed about that'. The stories have evolved a lot from that.

WJ: How have the stories evolved?
CL: WOW stories were originally about the customer so we'd say that they were very 'on brand' in terms of delivering a good brand customer experience. A lot of the initial stories were around staff doing things outside the scope of their roles but very much part of what they see as their job and the service they provide. Having very strong links in the community is part of our culture as well. A lot of the stories were things like people doing things after hours, really outside the scope. If someone leaves their card behind and they know they're going to the airport they'll take it to the airport. There were lots of those types of stories.

Then what we've found more over the last while is we were wanting to hear about how people were delivering on our business objectives as well. So it's not just the service part of the company but how they were fulfilling that customer's needs and the solutions they were providing to the customer. Stories about the tangible things that were being done to support that, and not just about leaving the customer with a smiley face. It became more planned about wanting to see the business objectives. The stories have gone through an evolution and you actually have to work to get the right sort of stories out.

Now we want to get back to hearing that customer voice because we've gone a little bit further with what we're doing for the customer, and not so much what the customer was saying about that. We're now going through a phase of refocusing people back to the day-to-day interactions. For example, simple things like it is really important that you remember to smile. That one second of interaction you have with the customer, that first point of contact, is 'it'. I think it's normal for it to be cyclical because we've been doing it for over four years now. This has been positive because it's making the stories fuller.

WJ: How do you share your stories and get them out there?

CL: WOW has always been very leadership-led. It started with Wayne Besant, our Head of Retail Banking, telling the stories. We have a WOW centre that collects people's stories. In the early days Wayne would publish these stories on the website and people were saying 'well I do that every day, so it's not really a WOW story'. We've done work around looking at how to get WOW stories that fill in the gaps that people miss. We'd ask them to think about what the customers think of that situation? What did it do to make that customer think like that? We've had to do quite a lot of helping to shape the WOW stories. We have a local manager in each of our local markets and they send out communications that will have a WOW story in them. Stories are in all our communication. The general managers and senior managers have electronic newsletters because the teams are all geographically spread from the top of the North Island to the bottom of the South Island. There's always a section that will have an example that will highlight things that our staff have done. So there's also a recognition piece to the sharing of the stories.

There's a framework that sits behind the WOW programme that involves a weekly Wednesday morning meeting in the branches. The meetings are themed and there's a good support structure around how that happens and what the focus is. A key aspect, that's been there since the beginning, is that we start or conclude the meetings with storytelling. It's open to all staff to share and it's the responsibility of whoever is running the session to have one up their sleeve if the team doesn't have one that week.

We have a story database so if any manager wants a story for whatever reason, they can access it. Anybody in the support team can go and find a story that links up from our frontlines. The database makes it easy for people to find an appropriate story. Our senior people don't need to go to the database because they get these stories sent directly to them. They wouldn't need to go hunting and we've never heard any of them say they've struggled to find something.

Another tool are the DVDs we use for the training and support that we provide for our staff. We have customers tell their stories and we'll use actors to play out scenarios based on real life experiences. Sharing stories this way is also a powerful medium when it comes to training.

WJ: How has having a structure such as WOW been important to the success of storytelling?

CL: It's very important and we're fortunate that we have this vehicle where we can provide these stories. We're able to utilize particular stories to really highlight other things that are going on. Some of that will be when we're launching information about well-being or support for our customers and staff. We will deliberately add stories from where people have been going through a financial crisis and the support they received. There's a good understanding about how we use it to influence people.

The WOW program is very specific to the aims of the retail culture. We're actually a large organisation made up from a lot of smaller businesses and there are differences around the cultures. Storytelling will be happening in other business units, it's just that we actually have a specific structure and a label around it. This makes it easier to articulate. For example, our global values have just been relaunched and having this deliberate structure gives a platform for our leaders to drive this cultural change.

Generally speaking, New Zealanders aren't very brave with telling their ideas to the group. So having this structure in the branches gives our people that security to share. Now people expect to see the sharing of ideas and stories from all levels. If we started sending a newsletter from a general manager without any stories in it, we'd get questions about what was happening. It's important because of that recognition piece that is attached to it when you're using your own staff or your own customers. People also learn from the stories too. They will ask, 'Am I doing that?' We've also had feedback over the years when people have said, 'That's not good enough!' and demand a higher standard.

Having a structure is important because you don't want to get complacent about telling stories. You actually have to actively encourage the storytelling and look for where we can get more opportunities from it. Sharing stories with our customers is equally important. It's a way to help customers in whatever situation. When we see people in financial hardship we can tell them, 'I've had a couple here in exactly the same situation as you, this is what we've put in place for them'. It's helping them understand that they're not alone.

WJ: What impact has WOW had?

CL: We know it's successful when we have other organisations coming to us and saying, 'we've heard about this programme, what is it?' Banking has been through a hard time but we're now passing what we call the BBQ test. If you were at a BBQ and someone asked you what you did work-wise, in the past, our staff would be embarrassed to say they worked for ANZ. Now they're very proud so sharing our stories has had a positive result in lifting our engagement levels with our staff. We have this discussion where we ask if we took away WOW now, what would happen? If we said to the guys they don't need to run the Wednesday morning sessions anymore, they'd still do it regardless.

Interview with Murray Jack

CEO of Deloitte New Zealand

Murray Jack initially commenced his role with Deloitte, one of the world's largest professional services' firms, as an auditor in 1976 and is now the CEO of Deloitte New Zealand. He has over 25 years as a management consultant and is a recognised expert in health policy, information systems, and industry issues. A chartered accountant, he is a member of the New Zealand Business Roundtable and has also served as a member of the Health Information Management and Technology Advisory Board.

WJ: What role does storytelling play here at Deloitte?

MJ: Storytelling is consciously in our DNA and we use stories a lot. We use them extensively around our learning and development programmes and as part of our messaging to get across our values. We use them in recruitment and in our graduate induction programmes. We'll share stories in the work that we do with clients, particularly in the advisory services area, where we use stories to convey prior relative experiences that clients can learn from.

WJ: Do you use stories yourself?

MJ: I do, particularly in graduate induction. Every year we recruit about 120 graduates and they go on our induction programme where we introduce them to the firm and what we're trying to do. We tell them how their career can unfold and what kind of options they have. I do an introductory piece in that program where I simply share stories based around my experiences and how I started as a graduate, the challenges I've faced and specific examples of the things that worked well and the things that didn't work well in my career. I tell the story of how my career evolved from what it was like when I joined, what I thought I'd be doing to what I ended up doing. Using your own career as a case study helps graduates understand the options that they might have should they wish to pursue them. We've found that these stories have been a very successful way of engaging people, particularly the younger ones, those people in their early 20s that are joining us.

WJ: Why do you think it engages the younger people?
MJ: I think it's relevant to them. Starting out they don't have a lot of well-developed concepts about what a career and a profession means and to hear from others that have been through the process helps them think about what they're trying to achieve, when they need to decide to commit to be a professional long-term in the firm, what the challenges involve, what the other options are, what to do to be successful. And it's not just the partners conveying their experiences – we also get previous years' graduates to do little talks about their experiences when they joined the firm and how their career has unfolded. We convert a bunch of those stories into podcasts which we make available to applicants and people who have decided to join us as part of the whole graduate recruitment process. We've had positive feedback and it's been an effective way of storytelling that works well for us.

WJ: What is your take on the role of storytelling in leadership?
MJ: I think effective leaders use storytelling as part of their suite of techniques that they have. I also think it comes naturally to a lot of leaders anyway, partly because they like talking about themselves and their experiences. These days, leaders need to be warm and stories help people to see their leaders as real people and not just some kind of bland image that emerges from behind a desk to make an announcement.

WJ: What about the role of storytelling and the organisation's values?
MJ: We have things called 'signals', which are like values and behavioural traits. We've got six of these signals and refresh them every few years, to ensure they stay relevant for our people. The signals stay the same but we change the imagery that goes with them and refresh the descriptors that fit within the particular signal to make the language more contemporary and

relevant. We used storytelling as part of the role of the relaunch when we relaunched them 18 months ago. We had partners talk about some of their specific experiences around a particular signal and sharing an example of how that signal had affected what they were trying to achieve at the firm. The partners would share these stories in person and over the internet. At this time we also ran a storytelling competition for each of the signals and had a panel of the wise and good to choose the best of the stories that were submitted.

WJ: Do you measure the impact of these initiatives?
It's difficult to know what sort of impact that sort of process has, as to whether it improves people's level of engagement or not. We don't measure it as such other than in a very indirect way through our manual engagement survey process, which we tend to score pretty well in.

WJ: How does the storytelling fit in with you sharing your vision for the organisation?
MJ: Rather than just having a statement there's dialogue behind it to give people a context of what it is that we're really trying to achieve, why we want to achieve it and what we're expecting. It's a narrative that explains why it is that we've chosen the particular vision that we have and what we need by its different components. I share this narrative in all sorts of forums, from our graduate inductions to our annual senior manager and associate director forum, where we revisit it to check on our progress.

WJ: How important is storytelling when it comes to knowledge sharing?
MJ: We use stories quite a lot in that area. Often they're brand-managing experiences that we may have had. We will use them again to illustrate to people the sort of things that they need to be aware of in protecting our brand. For example if we haven't followed a particular procedure policy because somebody thought it wasn't that relevant and subsequently it proved to be quite relevant, then as a result we had service delivery issues or they've taken on more significant business risk than we intended. Because we hadn't complied with our own policies and procedures we lacked the ability to control the reputational consequences of that. We use those stories when we're communicating with partners and our people the importance of

good judgement around compliance issues and so on. We use storytelling internally beyond the formal learning development environment around sharing the client success stories, for example where we've done something that we think is particularly good for the client. We share those stories on our own. Every week we'll have numbers of stories about how we've helped a client solve a particular problem, who was involved, how we went about it, what the outcomes were. That again is part of the knowledge sharing, the lifeblood of our organisation. It'll be shared in meetings, in emails and in formal reports. And these stories find a way outside our organisation. We don't do any formal advertising as our brand spreads by word of mouth, by the stories that people tell about us.

Interview with Michelle van Gaalen
Group Manager Retail, NZ Post

Michelle van Gaalen has been in her current role at NZ Post since 2006 and has held management positions with Westpac, Telecom and Bank of New Zealand. She has a diverse background in services-related industries in the disciplines of marketing, strategy, e-business, sales, and operations. She is also a Director/Trustee for Chamber Music New Zealand – a not-for-profit organisation dedicated to presenting quality chamber music throughout New Zealand, both from local and international artists.

WJ: Is storytelling important for you?

MvG: I find storytelling is really important in terms of the culture, the brand and for the people, especially working in quite a large organisation which is diverse, geographically and in a number of other ways.

One of the keys for me when I first came into the business was to get out on the front line and out to where our customers interact with our people, and find the stories which help to reinforce the behaviours and the direction and the culture that we wanted to create. Because it's all well and good for me to sit here and we all get the ivory tower analogy, but if you can actually go out and talk to people about stories that they can relate to because they have actually had the experience or seen someone else having the experience or something they do on a daily basis, it's a much more powerful way to get your message across. I could stand up there and talk about customer service, I could go out there and talk about the great experiences and our vision and our mission and our strategy too but to be able to link it into actual examples of conversations I've had with customers, conversations I've had with people, things that I have seen that are real live examples of where it's working really, really well, or where we can learn from, I find that engages people much more powerfully. You get much more, the lights go on in the eyes and the bodies lean forward and they laugh and they engage versus a set of PowerPoint slides around strategy and vision and so forth.

I've always found that storytelling was exceptionally powerful to engage emotionally with people because it's more relevant to them, it actually means more to them. And I pick people and I talk about people that they know. I talk about people at the front line that I've had conversations with and I talk about Wayne, or Mary, or John and so they know the people and they actually know that I understand them not just the theory of it. So that, to me, is really important and what you do find is that some of those stories become legends and they will be played back to you.

I also find storytelling, because of its power, a really nice way to get key messages out into the business that you want repeated. We were really clear here when we came in and we were working really hard to change the culture of the business in a certain direction. Everything was around getting a consistent story. We found through storytelling and the way we communicated with our people and still do in telling stories, not only verbally but through written communications, is that just after around ten months, the key messages started to come back to us. People learn and they communicate through words whether they are written or oral. We started to find the words coming back which was good because it actually meant that people were talking about it in a day-to-day way versus a vision and mission way, about things that were most important to our organisation and the direction we wanted to take.

WJ: Do you have an example of one of those stories?
MvG: We work in a business which is very high volume, we have a lot of customers – we serve 20 million customers a year through our post shops and one of the challenges for us is to make sure that we treat each customer as an individual, as each customer is different. We talk a lot about our purpose to create great experiences that our customers value. One of the challenges is when you have a high volume, there is a tendency as we all find when you're busy, to actually just get through the customers. What we

wanted to make sure was that our people were still thinking about what was important to each individual customer.

I have a story about a fantastic young guy who I have interacted with as a customer. He didn't know who I was, and it was a Saturday and I wanted to send a gift to Australia to friends of ours and I had to get the parcel out that weekend. I went and picked up a pre-paid Australian envelope off the wall and stood in the queue. I felt him meet my eye, thanked me when I got to the counter for my patience, he did everything perfectly. He made the experience positive, welcomed me warmly, everything was just fantastic around the service experience. And the first thing he said to me when I said I wanted to send something to Australia, he said 'You can do it cheaper another way', and I went 'yeah that's cool, but I want to take this away because I haven't got the gift with me and I have a card at home and some photos at work and I want to put it all together and just throw it in the mail in a post box on Monday'. And he said 'if you come back on Monday we can do it cheaper for you'. His intent was absolutely right, he wanted to give me the cheapest price because that's what he thought I valued.

What he wasn't hearing, what was valuable to me in this instance, was I could buy this and didn't have to come back. My time was valuable. I didn't want to have to buy a bag go home collect everything together and come back to the post shop. And so that was a story I told a lot about not assuming what the customer values but listening to what the customer says and understanding because in that instance to me, the most valuable thing was time and convenience. I was willing to pay $1 or $2 more for the convenience of not having to come back and stand in a post shop again to get it weighed. So when you get stories like that, it gets people to think about how to step back from what they think is most important and actually listen to the customer about what's important.

And we have stories about our people who do the most incredible things for our customers, it's amazing what people think that you can do once a 50 cent letter gets in the mail. The number of times we have told stories about staff who have been rung in the weekend by our call centre because tickets to a special show or a birthday present or something is in a PO Box or in the store somewhere and a customer is frantic to get it and our people have gone out of their way to go in and find that.

One story from central Auckland is where a customer accidently posted their passport and had to fly out that weekend. It was a tourist, an Asian customer and luckily one of our staff spoke the language. Our staff member went out of their way to find the passport and got in their car and took it out to the airport to the customer. And those stories, those experiences, customers value. We use a lot in terms of our enforcement and our recognition around that and the stories are just endless. The challenge is finding fresh ones because you can't use the same ones all the time.

WJ: How do you share these stories?
MvG: We do road shows once a year, there's our reward and recognition programme and we also have a whole series of written communications from our intranet site through to a newsletter or an update that I send out on a regular basis. We try very hard to use consistent language guidelines across all our communications so that the same key messages are put through consistently. So when we are trying to recognize or reward or talk about particular stories, we have phrases that we like to use and build into them so that we make the linkages for people through all different types of communication. We have our recognition stories, in our weekly or monthly newsletters we recognize people who have created great experiences that our customers value.

WJ: So when you share a story you'll link that back to common language?
MvG: Yes. For example 'creating great customer experiences' is a phrase that we will use consistently. It might be things that really helped, 'Mary really did what was right for the customer in that situation', she 'stepped out of the boundaries and did x, y and z', or 'John really did what was right for the customer because he went out of his way and made sure that his team members were doing what's right'. What we find over time is that it becomes embedded and ends up part of the culture.

WJ: Do you use storytelling yourself as far as setting the vision?
MvG: Yes, particularly when I go out and either talk at regional meetings or nationally. With everything I do I try to link back to our vision and where we want to get to. Storytelling is a really compelling way to do that. One of the things we do in our executive leadership team, at executive level from time to time, is we will actually do elevator speeches to each other saying if you got into a lift and you had to explain the vision and you had to explain what

retail was trying to achieve what would you say? You could say that's not storytelling, that it's just communication, but to engage the people you have got to make it a story. You know it has got to have a beginning, a middle and an end, and its got to have a message. Everyone's got their own words and their own way of describing it, but you get a sense of the key messages that are the same. When we go out and do national road shows, we make sure that the stories are all aligned. We will tell our stories to each other before; we will practice to make sure that happens. The only way to get the vision across is to tell the story. You can't just send out a document, or put a plaque on a wall, well you can, but we don't believe that is the most effective way to communicate to our people. We actually made a conscious decision to never put up our mission statements, vision statements or value statements.

WJ: The leadership team made this decision?
MvG: Yes. For retail, we have never gone out and put up posters on the walls or things for our people. We talk about it and we use it in communications, we use it in reports, we will use it, but it's not like we say to every store here are our values: put them on the wall. Our view is then it's just another poster on the wall and it becomes wallpaper. We believe that the most important way to do that is to make it part of the language.

At our last staff engagement survey we did, around 95% of our people could actually articulate the key messages from the vision and culture and strategy piece back to us. That's what we want, we want them to be able to play it back to us and that's what we were working to achieve. We didn't want them to point to a poster on the wall and say there it is. Very few of them can do it word for word, and that's fine by me. They can articulate the key elements of our vision and purpose back to us. I know we have made a significant move in the last three years about people who believe they understand where they fit in the organisational journey and that they understand where the organisation is going. It hasn't been about the poster on the wall as there are no posters on the wall, there's no collateral. It's actually been on culture and a lot of the culture has been around the stories and the language used in that piece.

WJ: Can you share with me any success stories?
MvG: People say we have quite an aging work force, and ask don't you need

to get a lot of young people? My view has always been it's not about age, it's about mindset. It doesn't matter how old you are, you can still learn. If you're in the right mindset, you can do anything. A story I use to make this point is actually quite a recent one. We are really good in this organisation about recognizing people who have worked for us for a long time. We have a dinner once a year celebrating people who have been in the company for over 35, 40 and 45 years. The executive team go and I was there talking to some of the retail people, having conversations with them about the value they have brought to the organisation. And of course a lot of them have seen significant change, as 35, 40, 45 years ago, we were a very different business than we are today. After the dinner I make a point of writing to them and their partners thanking them for coming and posting it to them at home.

One of the stories I've got now that came out of that was from a woman who was there. She made the effort of sitting down and writing me a letter back, which I still have. She wrote to me about what a difference that event had made to her and that she'd found herself starting to get a bit stale. She had been here over 35 years, and how the evening reminded her about how valuable the organisation was and how valuable she was within the organisation. She was talking to her manager about how she feels reinvigorated, and wants to learn and move on. I went to see her about a month after that, when I was down in that region, and she was saying to me she went to a BBQ one day and there happened to be an old postal worker who she knew from years back. He was saying to her 'it was much better in the old days' and she said 'no you're wrong, it's much better today, we get much better development and we get much more variety'. She said she feels like a different person and for me, this is a really good story about how you can take people on a journey no matter how long they have been in an organisation.

When people say we need a young workforce, I think of a manager of ours down in Christchurch. She was one of our first managers and has been in the organisation for over 40 years. She didn't come out of banking as the bank has only been part of our business for seven years, yet she came to us and said I want to be a lender. She was one of our first managers to have in-store lending added into her store, and at 65, she's doing a fantastic job. She's loving it and customers love talking to her because they're talking to someone who's got lots of experience rather than a pimply-faced 18-year-old. A lot of people who are looking for mortgage or home loan advice are actually older people. They are in their 30s, 40s or 50s, and to have someone who is more mature works for them. One of the big myths that I try to work on around here is 'You can't teach an old dog new tricks'. I don't agree with that at all. I collect stories around this because I think that it's really powerful to shift people's mindsets. Sure there will be some people who don't want to come on the journey, but they might be 20 just as easily as they might be 60. It's not about age, it's about the person.

WJ: Any stories of values in action?

MvG: We have a series of four, what we call touchstones, which is how we want our people to behave, how we want them to make decisions around what's right for the business. One of the touchstones is 'going further together'. Team is very important to us. We look for the stories around examples of that, of people that have come with really good ideas and then we have had them working on them. We had one only a few months ago. One of the challenges for us at Christmas is we get really, really busy with everyone sending Christmas parcels. We have all the counters manned and put people on the floor but you're still going to have queues. One of the challenges was how do we make that experience better for customers. There's a lot of things we do such as having floor workers, trying to sell stamps on the floor rather than behind the counter, but one of the challenges was people had already paid for their parcels, they had to queue to just drop it off. So one of the team here in the support office, and it wasn't part of their role, said, 'Can't we do a quick deposit box to find some way around that?' We said, 'Fantastic idea, go for it'. So they got a team together with people from our postal services group partners and within about two weeks they had brought together a process and a trial. I haven't seen the results yet, but within three weeks they had a trial out in key stores over Christmas to actually see if we could make this work effectively. It's a revenue protection issue for us so it's not just as easy as putting a big box out and letting people dump parcels in it as we have to make sure that they have put the right postage on it because once they've gone, you can't find them. They had to put a whole trial in place around that and they worked together as a team to try to create a much better customer experience and they had done it in about three weeks. It's a good story about our teams going further together.

Interview with Kevin Roberts
Worldwide CEO of Saatchi & Saatchi

Kevin Roberts has been the Worldwide CEO of Saatchi & Saatchi since 1997. He leads a team of 6,000 people across 150 offices in 86 countries. Saatchi & Saatchi have the reputation of being one of the world's leading creative organisations. Kevin is the author of *Lovemarks* and *Sisomo* and co-wrote *Peak Performance: Lessons for Business from the World's Leading Sports Organisations*. He holds Honorary Professorships at the University of Auckland Business School, the Peruvian University of Applied Sciences, and Lancaster University, England.

WJ: How have you used stories personally?
KR: I think it was Rolf Jensen of the Copenhagen Institute for Future Studies who said that the heroes of the 21st century will be the storytellers. Our whole culture here is based on storytelling. We are not driven by financials, we are not driven by The Balanced Scorecard, we are not driven by management buzzwords. Management, doing things right, is not the way you move forward. You move forward through inspirational leadership from every chair, from inspiring your people to be the best they can be. And you start by telling them a story of 'Purpose', and sharing the inspirational dream of the company. The focus of the company. The beliefs of the company. The spirit of the company. The stories that we tell in the company are all built around our Purpose, which in brief is about 'Nothing is Impossible'.

We have an ever-growing bank of Nothing is Impossible stories that we add to, that are on the net, that we tell each other, that we share with new people, and that we share with clients and prospects. We have stories that are partly legend, partly truth and partly fiction but all inspirational.

Our focus in the company is to fill the world with 'Lovemarks' so we have a lot of stories that are around about people's lovemarks. You can see all that happening on KR Connect where I tell a story every day. And it's a story about anything to do with Purpose. I don't tell stories that aren't relevant to the purpose of the company. So we tell the stories through KR Connect, we tell the stories through our website, we tell the stories through a thing called mysaatchi.com that everybody can go to. We are a unique company and we believe in the appeal of mystery. Lovemarks are driven by mystery, sensuality and intimacy and mystery is in all of our storytelling. The more you know about something the less interesting it becomes. So to keep people involved and engaged in the world we live in, we tell stories. If you can't tell stories at Saatchi & Saatchi, you can't succeed because the planners have to tell stories to the creative department, the creative department have to tell stories to consumers, the account guys have to tell stories to clients. For us, asking, 'Are stories important to Saatchi?' is like asking, 'Are computers important to Dell'? It's the same thing.

WJ: Are there any specific stories that spring to mind in regards to the impact the story has had on any of your team or your staff?

KR: Yes, I just spoke to the New Zealand agency in Auckland and I told them the story of my presentation two weeks ago. Two weeks ago I was in Radio City Music Hall, which is an iconic venue in New York, with 5,000 people in front of me, George Lucas from *Star Wars* about to follow me, and President Clinton about to follow him. So I told our people the story of how that felt and then I gave them the presentation that I actually made to 5,000 people in Radio City Music Hall. This morning I have just been inundated with emails about 'thanks for taking the time' and 'wow it was great to see how the big guys think' and 'it's great to get a feel for what the big issues are'.

Then with the same group, I gave them our 15 challenges for 2010 for the global network, not just for New Zealand. I illustrated stories around each one because most of them were not directly involving New Zealand. An example of storytelling in front of 90 people that lasted two hours. And I had fun at least!

I just spent the last hour filming for a documentary, *Cup of Dreams*, that's being made about the Rugby World Cup in New Zealand. I spent an hour telling stories about the power of the All Black brand, the heritage of the All Blacks, and why the All Blacks mean so much to me. So I've actually spent the entire day today telling stories.

Yesterday I spent 90 minutes telling stories to 15 entrepreneurs from the Entrepreneurs Organisation New Zealand, where I described what I have learned in business over 40 years. I didn't have any props and for an hour and a half these guys just lapped it up, wrote copious notes and asked loads of questions.

WJ: What's your take on the stories that get retold throughout the organisation?

KR: A great story becomes a legend. A larger–than-life story repeated many times. For example, when I was running Pepsi Cola, I machine-gunned a Coca-Cola vending machine. Now that story has become a legend and people talk about it wherever I am in the world. At the time we were in the cola wars and people thought you can't beat Coke. I was trying to make the point that Coca-Cola held no fear for me and I did it theatrically and dramatically. This story is told whenever I get introduced. It must be on a website or something, I don't know where it is actually, but that story, that legend crops up. Of course I didn't actually machine gun the thing. I had it all wired up and I fired blanks just to explode it, but everybody was convinced I shot a live machine gun in a 5-star convention centre. Even when I do point out it was blanks, it doesn't matter, they never repeat that part, truth never gets in the way of a good story.

When I was at Lion Nathan, I took a lion into an analysts' meeting and it certainly focused their attention. We had just put the words Lion and Nathan together and it was a new company so we wanted to get recognition and recall of the new name. They never forgot the name of the company after that.

WJ: Did the lion have a little name tag saying Nathan?

KR: It didn't but that would have been clever.

WJ: What's the most important story in business?

KR: To be purposed-inspired and benefit-driven. Martin Luther King did not say, 'I have a vision statement'. He had a purpose. He had a dream. Everything starts with purpose at Saatchi & Saatchi. We have a one-page purpose. All my stories are around that purpose and that purpose is shared with everyone, employees, prospects, clients, because if you don't buy into that purpose you can't work here. If you don't buy into that purpose you won't be a good partner because it talks about what we believe in. Our stories are around that purpose and when we share that purpose with people, we don't share it with them through PowerPoints or writings, we share it through stories. An example would be a Lovemark that we moved from a brand to a Lovemark and how we did that. One of the things we believe in is the Saatchi & Saatchi mystique and that's manifested via stories.

WJ: Can you give me an example?
KR: When I picked up the phone to speak to Kofi Annan at the United Nations he took the call straight away. Why? Because I was the head of Saatchi & Saatchi. Saatchi & Saatchi has brand power and fame beyond advertising because people believe we can deliver a Nothing is Impossible outcome. We helped to get Margret Thatcher elected way back in the UK with this great campaign called 'Labour isn't working'. Ask people in New Zealand how many agencies they can name? They always name Saatchi & Saatchi.

WJ: Can you give me an example that you might tell a potential Saatchi client, one story you might tell them where you took it from a brand to a Lovemark?
KR: JC Penney is one of the biggest department store chains in the United States of America. Two years ago I was speaking at a conference in downtown New York and the first speaker was Mike Ullman, the CEO of JC Penney. He spoke about leadership and I was really inspired. I was next on stage and spoke about Lovemarks. At the end of my presentation he said, 'Kevin this Lovemarks thing is fantastic. I want you to make JC Penney the most loved department store in America'. Twelve months later we were appointed to their business, which is a $300 million piece of business, without a pitch, because they were inspired by our Lovemark story. Two years later they are a Lovemark.

WJ: Do you find stories play an important part in selling in a brand?

KR: That's everything we do. For us it's an art form. Our core business is storytelling. And we've got great storytellers. The company's full of them as we make our living by selling and by telling stories. There's no more selling by yelling, it's all selling by telling stories.

WJ: Would you agree that everyone uses storytelling anyway, so let's use it consciously as it's a powerful leadership tool?

KR: Yes and stop using it sloppily. It pays to know your storytelling style. I see it in four categories. You're either a charismatic, creative, cartographic or cognitive storyteller. All the world is moving into the charismatic and creative styles yet all businesses are into cognitive and cartographic styles, that rely on charts, slides, facts and figures. This is made even more so by the internet and PowerPoint. Charismatic and creative styles is where the action is because this is where you get engagement. People get engaged, they look, they listen, and they learn in this space. This is where the storytelling has got to be. Cynical, personal criticism and a lot of the negative stories are not condoned at Saatchi.

WJ: Do you see stories as a reflection of a company's culture?

KR: Absolutely. Proctor & Gamble is a company that tells a lot of stories about success because at the top of P&G's values is winning. So if winning is at the top of your thing then you tell a lot of stories about winning. The All Blacks are not about winning, the All Blacks have a fear of losing so all the stories that Sean Fitzpatrick tells are about when they lost and how bad that feels.

Stories have got to be in context and have a message otherwise they are bewildering to people. Like you, I think storytelling is the most powerful way to inspire people to be more productive. I think telling stories makes people happy and I think happy people work harder. There is a really direct chain in this thing, I'm not telling stories because I am a storyteller, I can do that at night-time. I tell stories to inspire people to perform at their peak.

We don't tell negative stories; I think that's really important. What we don't want to have in our culture are negative stories of 'don't do that', as we think that's uninspirational. We tell stories that are all about engaging people positively. We don't tell fear stories, retribution stories, we don't tell stories that have bad consequences, we tell stories that are emotional, that are purpose-driven and that are designed to provide learning and recognition.

There are four words that drive us in every story: responsibility, learning, recognition and joy. So in every story we try to make clear to the person that we're telling it to that it's their responsibility to do something with this story. The reason I'm telling this story is so you will do such and such. You're going to learn something in this story otherwise I wouldn't waste your time. I am going to recognise in this story that you're a good player that I rate you very highly. And I'm going to give you some joy out of this story not fear. So everything we try and do has those four elements. Every story should have an element of responsibility, learning, recognition and joy in it. That's what inspires peak performance.

Interview with Roger Bell
CEO of Vero Insurance

Roger Bell has been involved with Vero Insurance for 33 years and has been Chief Executive since 2007. He sits on the Board of the New Zealand Business Excellence Foundation and is a member of the New Zealand Business Roundtable. In 2008 Vero became one of only two companies in New Zealand to ever achieve the gold standard in the Baldrige Criteria for Performance Excellence, an international best practice framework oriented towards commercial success, making Vero Insurance a world-class company.

WJ: What do you think of when you think of organisational storytelling?
RB: Instead of making speeches, good leaders tell stories. I think it puts colour into what you're saying. It's also authentic because you're telling people about real stories that happened in the company or in a market environment. I think in our induction programme, for instance, one of the biggest themes we would have promoted over the past 10–15 years was our path to gold. Secondly we talk about how almost all players in our market lose money on their core business, and to draw a distinction between their strategy and ours. Typically what they have is an absence of strategy. They follow market rates downwards to the lowest level and then they go out of business. The most dramatic point I can make to our staff is that when I started we had 40 competitors, and now we're down to four. It's an astounding story, saying that those were all good companies, and a lot of them were household names, a lot of them we ended up buying. In the end

they didn't run their business, they allowed the market to run their business and that's the absence of a strategy. So that puts colour around that idea and really brings it home for the staff.

Another way I've used it effectively, and it's a very touchy subject, like any big company when you survey your staff the good news is that we rate very highly for staff engagement and confidence in the leadership, values, and pride. But like any company if you look at the lower scores you will always see that the remuneration is fair. There are two things driving that. Everyone wants to be paid more, and secondly they harbour views that there are other people who get paid more than them and that's unfair. People just automatically think that. What I've done with stories is actually to confront every group of staff members and say to all of them, 'I want some questions, this is my time in front of you'. I say, 'Let's get it started, who thinks our salary's fair?' A few hands go up. Depending on the audience I get a good response. Then I say, 'Pretend you're in my seat', and people say, 'We made good profit, I think I should get paid more'.

So the next group would be the shareholders who are saying that they want world-class dividends, then the pensioners want more. Then the insurance brokers come to us and want more commission. Then the last of the queue would be the customers who are getting charged through the roof and want lower premiums. By the time I go through the story people giggle about the notion that if they were doing my job they could keep everyone happy. 'We consider a world-class approach is to benchmark your base salaries at the median level of the market then we pay the better performance considerably better than that. Do you want to debate that with me? This is a good place to do that'.

Back to that story about the competitors, when I talk to the new people about how I had 40 competitor companies when I started, I also say, 'Do any of you want to make an argument that we should adopt their strategies?' We could be the best insurer in New Zealand with no customers left, because NZ companies and clients typically want cheap brackets. So does anyone want to make an argument? Then I make the argument I would only need half the people I've got because that's all I could afford. It's over here the strategy is world class, there are happy people with a good salary or over there we could become cheap and nasty. I say that we could be the cut-price model which is what our competitors are doing. Their problem is that they don't have any advantage, there's no logic about why they're cheaper than us. One day there'll be tears. And those companies have hit the wall big time now.

There's a third type I tell, which is with our path to gold and business excellence. I say, 'I know what you're thinking, what did this cost?' I say that I remember 20 years ago when we reported in to London and there were some very nice gentlemen on the board who say, 'Your profits are world-class why would you want to change anything?' They thought that because I was world-class I would put profits at risk but in fact it was the opposite. And I said to them that if they had better customer attention, more engaged service, better claims service, etcetera, by definition you will make stronger financial returns not less. I tell this story to all my audiences. That it's not a cost, you're enabling people to do things at the world-class level, and it will cost you not to do it. If times are grim then this is where you should do it and not worry about the cost of it. Therefore when my boards say to me now I've got to world-class standards, will I let people go, I say, 'But it's the staff who are doing the work. The staff are being able to do what they do at a world-class level.'

I share this story frequently with my staff.

WJ: How do you do that?
RB: We introduced a fabulous part of our strategy deployment called 'Cascade'. It's a company getting better at telling stories to its people because there's that old chestnut about how you align your staff with your strategy. We believe that you do that by being inclusive and making them feel part of the strategy, but how do you do that? We use this Cascade process. Every four weeks we have a day-long meeting of the executives. In that meeting we monitor our progress to strategy, our successes, the issues we've got that are preventing us getting to strategy, we have presentations from people who have got issues, we review our balance score cards, etcetera. I give a report from upwards, from our parent company because I attend their board meetings. We also discuss our monthly results. The minutes from that then go to every business unit, and we have about 68 of those. People prefer to get the message about the company from their leader, as they engage more when it comes from them. They want to see the group-wide performance in the context of their division.

The first part of the Cascade they receive are the minutes, which are boiled down to major briefings on the way our parent and Vero NZ are travelling towards its strategic plan. Then they report to a group of staff that have a meeting and we've given them a chart where they write what these major points are. This chart's in the staff room and that's what they sit around when they get their Cascade meeting. Then the unit leader writes in their contribution to the month's progress and they align their results with what they've seen for the group. It's showing the groups' profit, growth, return on capital, etc. They all report on their contribution to that and we also have a section on their achievement so they're celebrating in the team. They highlight the people in their group for the month that succeeded, gave great ideas, or extra special customer service. Then they lodge up their promises to the group of the things they will be achieving to make their contribution to strategy. So we've captured our stories, successes and issues, and these are documented and cascaded downwards. This Cascade goes to literally every staff member. We consider this to be priceless. In those cascade meetings they're telling their stories too and it works powerfully.

The other thing that happens a lot in our company is what place does humour play in a business? I believe it's very powerful. If you think of a culture of a company you've got a lot of serious things happening at work, but if you said to your staff what is it you love about your job most people will say it's the humour, the people, the crazy personalities. They say it with a lot of affection. On every day of my career somewhere we've stood around and laughed about the hard cases and the crazy stories.

WJ: Can you share a story?
RB: I was in a meeting on Friday and one of our guys had been to see some farming clients. He knocked on the door and they didn't answer, so he went round the back and there was a couple lying there naked having their cigarettes. They never really saw him, maybe they'd had something to smoke. He didn't know what to do so he put his business card between the guy's toes and he snuck out. There are just hundreds of such stories about the terrible things that happen. Those stories infiltrate your company and people not only laugh they also want to hear the story again. It reinforces the notion that they work with interesting people. They repeat the stories they heard at work, those legendary stories.

I have another recent one. One of my young guys did marathons and he ran a company that only served over 50s. We went to Taupo to do one of those corporate events and it rained so the outdoor activity had to go indoors. They used an event organisation to use a new event centre and they put these competitive team events together. This guy, despite his running marathons, collapsed and went blue in the lips. We called the ambulance. The first thing they do is they cut off your clothes and put you in one of those smocks. They thought it was a virus but there's an irregular heartbeat. They wanted to put him in observation and they had to put him in the geriatric ward. He said, 'Bugger, I'm back with these geriatrics and I don't have my cards!' I went back to the management conference and they were all really concerned about their friend. The boss stopped the conference and asked me for an update. I told the story with a straight face. I think these stories are not just stupid stories, they become part of the culture.

WJ: How can people use these stories that permeate the culture to consciously reflect the values?
RB: I like to use the Warren Buffett story, 'When the financial tide goes out you can see who's swimming in the nude.' I tell this story to our staff to say how people survived. His basic proposition is I don't invest in them because I don't understand them. So he bought companies like Coke and McDonalds because he understood them, and look who's laughing now! I tell this to say that in this industry you will get slightly ridiculed at times for working for Vero because we refuse to slash our prices, because idiots do. 'When the financial tide goes out you find out who's swimming in the nude'. Our competitors have been slashing prices because they don't have a strategy. I tell the story so they'll be confident that this company knows what it's doing. Every now and then people will get nervous because we're losing a bit of business and I'll say that we are but they're winning business on price so they'll lose it on price.

I travel through the country all the time so I can relay stories. Somehow if you said that to them in a manual it wouldn't always work. I never say to our staff to not write down risk. I don't have to because of our staff engagement. Our staff care. I see one of our main competitors published staff engagement and it's very low. It's at the level that is called the 'indifferent zone'. For one of the departments the level is in the 'destructive zone' so those people will hurt you if they get the chance. Every year we get offered those risks and

130

we turn them down and then the weaker competitors insure them. My point about the stories is that I then broadcast this across the staff. I tell stories like this to our business partners and our board. It gives the colour between the facts. The facts tell them that we're profitable when our competitors are not but the stories tell them why.

WJ: You use storytelling to impart the values as well.
RB: Yes. Two days after the values were introduced I had three stories and I broadcast these around the nation internally and externally. One story was that one group found that we had overcharged a motorcar premium. Someone had found a tiny problem. They said they'd undercharged or overcharged by no more than $5 for quite a few clients. The good news is they don't know. We could put it right on a renewal. We've got a value of integrity. I asked what the cost would be. Where we've overcharged it would cost $340,000. I asked what their recommendation was and they said that if we were true to our values we'd "fess up'. They wrote to all the clients apologising for overcharging them the amount. They added in a petrol voucher to the value.

Another story which we like to advertise is to give our staff confidence. Almost every week somewhere in NZ one of our managers will be meeting with our staff and say they have a problem and what they're going to do. Then a staff member will say that it sounds average. And the manager will say, 'Oh, bugger'. These stories encourage staff to hold their managers to upholding the values and being world-class. I always end the staff inductions by saying to our staff that the values mean we won't condone bullying, harassment, sleazy behaviour. We won't know unless you tell us. My big request to you is to remember that. If you hold us to account then you are holding yourself to those values. The story is to make them understand that we are real and we live the values. They won't get in trouble if they report us.

I have a story around this. A fairly senior guy who was an assessor had been with us for 15 years. We organised an in-house conference in Christchurch for all of our assessors. The manager specifically said that they would be in a hotel and not to use the mini-bar because the company will host for dinner and buy wine there. The guy doesn't turn up to the group dinner and the manager takes little note until the credit card bill comes in. There's an outfit in Christchurch on the bill on the night he disappeared. It was a strip bar, and the bill was for $150. They bring him in and ask what the expense was for. He said he had a few colleagues with him and they went to a club and he treated it as a business expense. He couldn't say who the colleagues were. The manager asked all of them and they said they didn't go with him. They said to the man that he breached two of the rules. One of them was integrity because he didn't show up. He then lied about it and tried to include his colleagues in the lie. They sacked him.

We don't deserve any credit for that, it's just what a good company would do. He called a few months later and couldn't get a good job because he couldn't tell other companies why he left Vero. He took us to court and wanted $80,000 for humiliation. I say to my staff to think about integrity now. He wants 80 grand. Do I want Vero on the front page for losing in an employment dispute because we sacked him on the spot and didn't give him a letter asking him to not go to a strip club? We decided it would be morally wrong to give him money. They lodged the proceedings. I ask a lot of our staff who thought we did the right thing, and all the hands go up. He came back to us and said that he wanted $20,000 but the lawyers would cost more than that. We said, 'No' on principle. Half the hands go up when asked if we did the right thing. So some people think it's a purely commercial issue, we're going to give $20,000 to a lawyer when we could give $20,000 to him.

He came back and said that he'd accept $5000 and we said, 'No', and no hands went up, because they're commercial people. We went to court and he never turned up. When it's a moral issue this company won't compromise. Because you read in the paper that Joe Blog's Ltd got taken to court and had to pay. Can you imagine how humiliating it would have been to reinstate that guy after we lost in court, to watch him walk in after six months and dropping hints to his colleagues that he won. It comes down to morality at a lot of different levels. It says that we won't just tolerate that behaviour we will also pay to stand up for what we consider is right.

WJ: When do you tell these types of stories?
RB: At every staff function. Every year I speak to every single staff member ranging from our small offices to our larger ones in Auckland. I don't use PowerPoint or stand up the front. I chose 10 years ago that we run focus groups to see what the staff think, and ask for questions, for anonymous feedback, and I also do a random phone-out to 20 of our staff. My secretary

goes into the page directory and gets a random selection by geographical distribution, age and department. I ring them up and say they can't get off the phone until they tell me something that we can do better. I use their colleagues' stories to give the exchange credibility to show the stories of the company, so I can find out if they agree or disagree. Then they start talking. I've been doing that for about eight years. I take note and jot down what people say so I can put them into action.

One other story I tell our staff is that one day I went to the Dunedin office about 3 years ago and asked the staff what we could do better. One woman suggested why don't we give something to people who have been here for a long time. I left that office and by the time I'd got to Timaru I'd done it. We could do it in the next week and it would cost about $100,000. We'd rung up Michael Hill jewellers, airlines, balloon companies, wine tours as we wanted to get things that people wouldn't usually buy themselves. The beauty of the story is two fold. One is to say to staff that if you have a suggestion we do listen. The second is that if it's a good suggestion it will happen. This company is committed to doing the right thing. Within two hours it was policy. It gives them the colour.

Every induction programme starts with introducing me and shows a picture of me in a suit. This is also when I talk to all our staff and brokers and when I talk to audiences who want to know about our path to Gold. With regards to the picture of the suit I tell them that I dress like that about twice a year, then I flick to the next picture and it shows me as Elvis, then Indiana Bell, my take on Indiana Jones. There are five altogether. I think that's a story with pictures because then I'm able to say to the audience that it's not about showing how much of a clown I am, there's a serious part to this story.

Why did we go to casual dress 10 years ago? Because we went open plan. We talked to staff 10 years ago in focus groups and moved from a management philosophy to a leadership one. We interviewed our staff and said we wanted to shift the emphasis from having managers to leaders. A young man put his hand up and said, 'Roger, you wear $1,000 suits and I don't even have a suit, you sit in a nice office and I sit out in the open, how can we make everyone part of the same team?' Within a few days we went open plan and dress-casual. I work in an open-plan office, people wander by and so I'm part of the grapevine. The Elvis thing shows that we actually have fun. How many staff members plan and pay to have fun? At Vero we do. That story sows seeds of us having fun and not taking ourselves too seriously; when we say we're going to have some fun with the organisation we actually do it. This is a story we tell a lot. I would have shown those pictures to thousands of people outside our company while trying to explain the culture of Vero that got us to Gold.

WJ: Can you tell me about where you've shared these stories recently?
RB: I've just done one for an outfit which promotes business excellence and I was the key speaker. The Haye Group, which is an international consultancy, ran a seminar from 9am to 12 noon and you had to pay $550 to come along. There were two Harvard professors on leadership and me. The professors each talked for about 30 minutes then I had about 2 hours. I agreed with the academic perspective but I talked about putting it into action. I was showing them the pictures and explaining them. The Indiana Bell one was launching a path to Gold. Why Indiana Bell? It's me as Indiana Jones. My whole executive group were Edmund Hillary, Christopher Columbus, as we're going where nobody had ever been before. I was saying to them that we had our executive team dressed as great explorers, and were taking Vero where no New Zealand company had been before and we were asking our staff to come with us. No New Zealand staff had gone where we're going. We need to find new ways of doing things, because we can't copy other NZ companies. I came out on stage with the whip, the old gun and the hat but then I talked about strategy. I said what the strategy would mean for people. It would have been threatening to some people but we told them to relax because we have a world-class framework. We used stories to deliver serious subjects.

WJ: Research shows that there are few companies paying to have fun.
RB: I bet in many company documents they say they are a fun organisation but they don't do anything about it. What we are proud of is planning to have fun and then paying big money to have a fun experience. For example our legendary Christmas parties. We had 580-odd people in the Vector arena and we had a riot of fun with our staff. We had a world-class theme so we wanted to celebrate Gold. We took that show to Hamilton, Palmerston, Wellington and Christchurch. In that show we employed some comedians who hosted it and we ran it as a world-class celebration – there was cuisine from the four corners of the world; American, African, Asian and European. In the

American corner we had a real bucking bronco, in the African corner we had African drums that you could learn to play, the Asian corner we had a Sumo suit and in the European we had breaking plates. Every couple of minutes we had a Trivial Pursuit question on each of the continents, we had modern music playing from each of the countries. Everyone was asked to come in a costume from around the world. We had prizes for the best dressed. There was a business theme to it. The theme was the fact that we've cracked the world-class thing and there was a trophy handed round to every staff member so they could kiss it. It was making it real for them. We had a lot of fun and there was a lot of humour. As I put the trophy on each person's lap they wanted their picture taken with it. It becomes part of our mythology and the stories continue.

Interview with Marie-Ann Billens
General Manager of Estée Lauder Companies

Marie-Ann Billens has been with the Estée Lauder Company for 20 years. The company is the largest prestige cosmetics company in New Zealand and its brands are Estée Lauder, Clinique, Aramis and Designer Fragrances, M·A·C, Bobbi Brown, La Mer and Jo Malone. Marie-Ann is a Trustee of the New Zealand Breast Cancer Foundation, a foundation that Estée Lauder Companies was instrumental in establishing 10 years ago. Philanthropy is very much part of the company culture and in New Zealand, the M·A·C Aids Fund has raised more than NZ$1 million since its inception in 1999. Marie-Ann is also the Chair of NAPTA Charitable Trust and a loyal supporter of Zonta, Auckland.

WJ: How important is storytelling in your organisation?
MB: We tell stories a lot and I suppose that's where we're different from many other companies as everyone who works for the company, whether they're a beauty adviser or here in the office, knows the story associated with the history, how their brand was born, its DNA and what makes their brand special and unique. For example, anybody who works for the Lauder brand knows the story of the founder, Mrs Estée Lauder, basically going door-to-door, selling in hair dressing salons, with the idea that she would put the product on the person in the hairdressing salon because they couldn't escape as they were sitting there under a dryer.

We communicate our values through our stories. Loyalty is very, very important to our organisation so everyone knows the great story about Mrs

Lauder getting her first order with Saks 5th Avenue. She sat in the reception area waiting to see the cosmetic buyer for Saks all day. People came and went and she wasn't called in and at the end of the day the buyer came out and she said, 'Seeing as you're still sitting here, come in and I'll see you.' Apparently the buyer's child had bad skin and Mrs Lauder gave her something to take home and put on it. It made such a difference the buyer said, 'Yes, we'll have you', and that's why Saks 5th Avenue is our flagship store. If you go to the Lauder offices you can see their first order framed in the doorway. And because Saks 5th Avenue gave her the first commercial opportunity, they always get the first of everything, the best of everything, and my understanding is we make no money from that store at all because we pretty much pay for everything. But they gave her the first opportunity and loyalty is important.

We can inspire through our stories and with Mrs Estée Lauder there are so many stories. One thing we certainly tell everybody is how she started the whole concept of 'gift with purchase'. She would give these ladies who were sitting in the hair salons a little packet, a little sample of something to take home and try. She went to an advertising agency who laughed at her, as they didn't think she had enough money to advertise so that's when she started saying if you purchase, you'll get a gift. She put all the advertising money into samples and offered a gift with purchase of her best-selling product and now of course, 'gift with purchase' has become a phenomenon. These days you get a gift with anything, any purchase, any brand.

WJ: How do you share these stories within the organisation?
MB: They're very much part of the induction but also the ongoing education of people. We probably see it mainly in the training of our beauty advisers and consultants, but even if you go to regional meetings you'll hear these stories coming out. It re-emphasises our history and shows us why we're doing some things today – it's based on the decisions we made years ago. We often find when a new advertising concept is presented, they will always show visuals and advertisements from previous years and it could be 20, 30, or 40 years ago where they've taken the inspiration from. It may be a piece of jewellery or the creative direction from that advertisement. You can go on to our international marketing website and see the development of Estée

Lauder through there because you can look at the beautiful visuals of ads that they've developed all the way through.

So many stories about our brands have just become engrained. And it's not just stories but also phrases. We may have set up a counter or set up for an event and we'll ask each other the question 'Does it look like Estée Lauder?' Mrs Lauder herself used to say, 'There's no ugly women only lazy women', and had a wonderful line, 'Telephone, telegraph, tell a woman'. There's a Clinique saying that says, 'It's not about looking young it's about looking good'.

Because the Lauder family is involved, it's a family business and you're part of that family. There are many stories around Estée Lauder but at the moment there is a quite a lot of focus on Leonard, Mrs Lauder's eldest son who is in his late 70s. Of course he's got so much experience to share with people and there is great concern that once Leonard passes we won't have these stories around. I was at a conference earlier this year and there was a great call for the stories to be written down, as we want to make sure that we've got these stories available to share with people. One of our big concerns would be with a lot of turnover of staff and a lot of new people coming through, we would have to ask, 'Do people know the stories'? These stories are so powerful, it builds loyalty not only from your consultants but also from your customers. And we really want to make sure that the stories are coming through and that they're remaining true without being embellished.

WJ: What are some of the stories that show the DNA of the different brands that your staff would know and share?
MB: The M.A.C brand has a lot of stories. It started when the two Franks, as they're called, couldn't get what they wanted. So they started making cosmetics up in one of their mother's kitchens and it spread through word of mouth. They never did and still don't do any actual advertising for that brand because it's just been built through people. For example, Madonna used M.A.C red lipstick on her worldwide tour and then everybody wanted that red lipstick and that's how the brand developed.

So many brands started in kitchens. Bobbi Brown started because she couldn't find the right foundation when a photographer took a photo at the shoot and the face was a different colour to the body. So she started making her own warm-toned, yellow-toned foundations. She also started off with 10 lipsticks, which she created herself, went into Saks and asked, 'Can I sell these lipsticks', and they said, 'Sure.' They gave her a little table, she put it by the door and she thought she'd sell 100 lipsticks in the month; she sold 100 lipsticks in the first day.

I remember Mrs Lauder saying when they first started out she would answer the phones and so she'd be the receptionist and then they'd say, 'Can you put me through to the training department', and she'd put the phone down and she'd go to another phone and pick that up and go, 'Training department', because they were so small but she just wanted them to know that they were very serious about their business.

Our stories put a very human face on what we do. We're in an industry where it's very, very competitive and we know that if we're really honest there are lots of very good brands out there. People relate more to something that they have empathy and a connection to and I think that's what the stories do. It turns the brand into a real thing rather than talking about just the ingredients. Some of the stories about how you develop the brand or wonderful stories about what a difference it's made to certain people, is something people can relate to. And certainly we use across all the brands a lot of examples of clients writing letters to us saying, 'I bought something for the very first time, to be very honest I was very sceptical but I just can't believe it', or 'I don't normally write letters but I felt compelled to write and tell you'. Those are very, very powerful to employees.

WJ: You tell those stories to employees?
MB: Yes we do. I can give an example about one of our consultants recently. I was in a store and she was telling me about this large sale that she had and this woman had come in and was very sick. Sue did her makeup and skincare and I think the woman was in tears. The woman's husband came back in to see Sue the next day to say that she had no idea the impact she had had on his wife. Here's somebody who had been through a lot of illness, obviously not a lot of self-confidence and now she was a different person to the extent that her husband took the time to drive to the store, come in and find Sue to say, 'You cannot believe the impact you had on my wife'. And I have told that story to a lot of people to inspire confidence and to reinforce the power of the product.

WJ: Do the staff use the stories with customers?

MB: Yes, particularly with fragrance. Every time we train in it we would talk a little bit about ingredients but every fragrance has got a story. The inspiration for the bottle would have been this dress, the white sleeves and the black dress, it's very powerful. That's primarily where we use it with our consultants and artists and beauty advisers as a selling tool, as much as to inspire and motivate them. Even Erin Lauder's keeping that going with the launch of the new private collection. She's delved into her grandmother's folder about this fragrance she was working on but never finished. So she's finished it but she's made sure she's put blue into the packaging, which was Estee's favourite colour, and she's picked up little bits and pieces of Estee and carried it to now, made it modern, which I think is great. They've used that story because that's not just another fragrance that we've launched, it's a fragrance with a whole history and story.

WJ: How about stories within the international organisation?

MB: Certainly at the moment, for the first time ever, we have a company strategy which is linked to our brand's strategy. In the past we had a company strategy, we had a mission statement and goals and then each of the brands had their own specific strategy, which was interpreted in different ways in different markets. And I think the company strategy was very much the big picture, no doubt about it, but there was not often the link between the brand strategy and the company strategy. We've got a new worldwide CEO now and he's all about strategy and cascading it down and cascading it up, and you're under no illusion as a company, as a brand, as an affiliate about what we need to achieve. He tells lots of stories to get the strategy across and the communication is constant, with videos coming out with him talking about his vision for the company. So communicating this vision to everyone in the organisation, telling the story, and they come out on a quarterly basis or whenever he's got news. Everyone in the organisation has access to these presentations through the intranet.

I've been with the company 20 years and remember when it really was a family company and now we are this big global company. I think it would be very, very easy to lose that DNA of what makes this company so great and this is also where the storytelling comes in. There's a story I tell many, many times. Leonard and Evelyn Lauder were here for a royal visit about eight years ago and we had hundreds of beauty advisors gathered at the Hilton. The Lauders could obviously tell there was an air of not only excitement but probably nervous anticipation as well, as people were quite concerned with what questions might be fired at them. They probably do it every time they speak to a group, but Mrs Evelyn Lauder was speaking and she was talking about doing work for breast cancer charity and how it makes you feel good doing something for other people, giving back, and it releases endorphins and she said, 'It's a bit like great sex before breakfast'. And Leonard looked at her and she looked at him, the whole room could not believe she'd said that and everyone relaxed and he said, 'Evelyn I told you not to say that'. It was just priceless. It may be a standard line they use once a week, but it was delivered perfectly, and it relaxed the whole room and showed they were just two people. I think this story humanises the company. It gives this global company that's focused on profitability the ability to keep its human face and makes it somewhere where people want to work.

Interview with John Harvey
Partner, PricewaterhouseCoopers

John Harvey has been with PricewaterhouseCoopers for over 36 years and a partner for 23 years. He was appointed Auckland Managing Partner in 1998 following the global merger between Price Waterhouse and Coopers & Lybrand, a position he held for over 8 years. John has also held various other governance and management roles, particularly in the Human Capital area, within PWC. Since 1998 PWC has become recognised as a leading firm in NZ and globally with a reputation for quality and excellence in all aspects of its operation.

WJ: What comes to mind when you think of storytelling?
JH: Storytelling is in the culture, and the way to live your career. We have this initiative, which is a very original sounding name – the PWC Experience. The PWC Experience is a global name but it's really trying to say we want both internally and externally people dealing with our people to have a good experience, and the internal and external focus is very important. Because it is set around behaviours, telling the story of what you're setting out to achieve is a very important part of that. The way you behave and get on internally should be no different to what you do with the way you get on with the clients. You shouldn't just be on your best behaviour when you go out and meet clients, it should be just PWC behaviour. So you give your client a PWC Experience. There is a business benefit from that perspective. In the training for the PWC Experience behaviours, you're not trying to convert people into new beings, into standard PWC beings. You're trying to capitalise

on their individual strengths. But a lot of that is coming back and being able to tell the story of positive experiences you've had and how you can convert that to another situation that you might be faced with. And we sit around in groups that are not just partners within the firm but are people typically arranged from graduate all the way through to partner, typically eight or nine people. And they're working together on that and it's been very effective. Graduates have been getting partners to talk about stories about some of the key experiences they've had. And what have been the determinants of the success or failure of that experience.

WJ: How long is the training?
JH: It's really ongoing. I guess we had a real campaign in the early part of last year. It was monthly sessions. Now it's cut back, most groups are getting together three-monthly or so. We're trying to keep those groups together so there is a camaraderie that's developed. The strength of it has been that it is across the entire firm.

WJ: How do you use storytelling personally?
JH: I tend to use it, in these sessions, or in a client-planning session from an intelligence perspective, to be able to draw on experiences that you've had to tell the story of that experience. It lets people draw the messages out of that. Hopefully you are pushing them in the right direction with those messages. Most of them are relationship-based. But to be able to give some real-life practical experience stories of maybe a situation you were faced with and how you overcame it, or a relationship challenge you might have been faced with and how you overcame that, and by them hopefully picking up on that so it can help them with their own development. I find I do most of my storytelling in an informal setting, one on one. A lot of that storytelling is facilitated around the subtleties as well. Because there was a time when you'd only do that in your office or in a meeting room, in a formal sort of environment. Whereas now the encouragement very much is, 'Why don't you take the person you're coaching down to level four and have a cup of coffee, sit in a comfy chair, just have a chat?' So trying to encourage people to create environments where it can be a much more relaxed exchange of stories.

WJ: How are stories used in the organisation to impart the values?

JH: We don't have the values up on the wall on a plaque, it's something that's very much installed in people right from day one when the graduates come in the door. The first part of the training is focused around either directly or indirectly teaching these people the values and behaviours of being part of a brand like PWC. In the organisation clearly relationships are very important, but you've also got to be able to stand back and make hard calls from time to time. I've had some situations in an internal environment that I can relay to people. From an official point of view you've got to have particular standards that you as an individual live by, and if that person who might have been a great mate of yours for five or six years is doing something that you can't agree with you've got to be prepared to stand up. There are some very good examples where we've done that. It's a very difficult thing for people to do, but if they can hear the stories of how this has happened in the past and relate to the individuals that were involved and realise that a) They can do it themselves and b) That they aren't on their own and that there's a firm behind them. That's been a pretty powerful thing in older partners like myself with younger partners, in giving them the strength to develop.

WJ: How about telling stories outside the organisation?

JH: From an external point of view you're trying to find a connection with clients, and if you're just going out there trying to sell something, you're not going to succeed. So if you can go out there with quite a story behind you, a lead-in, to what at the end of the day is going to be a sale then you're more likely to come away with success. I guess particularly in the current tough economic environment there are situations where you can talk about examples of other companies that have gone down a particular path, which may have a public profile. You may be selling it as a good path or as a bad path to achieve your goals. The stories are pretty powerful.

WJ: When do your people in the organisation tell stories?

JH: Depending on the nature of it, it may just be within that business unit and we have lots of different tiers within peer group meetings. We ensure that at those different levels that if there's been something really good happen that the story of that event is told at those meetings. We used to be hopeless at sharing success stories. We shared stories when we lost a proposal, but did nothing when we won one. We've got a lot better at celebrating successes, telling the stories about those successes and how we got there.

WJ: Can you give me an example of a success story that has been shared?
JH: We had a major client-win recently which we regarded as quite a coup because it was a large one and it meant that we were knocking out another big firm from the client. So we were pretty keen to tell the story. There was quite a team of people involved in bringing that and it was a one-firm team. Meaning it was a team made up of all people of all different parts of the practice. It wasn't just a tax win, it was bringing all these people together to win the assignment so we were pretty keen to sell that as a one-firm success story. So we didn't just have partners going to the peer group meeting, it was very much people at their level who were involved and were telling how the whole process worked. We were making sure we were selling the success to partner groups, to manager groups, and staff below the manager.

WJ: Was this an informal thing to tell the story?
JH: No, it was just part of regular meetings that these groups would have. So members of the one firm would come in and share the news. A couple of years ago this wouldn't have happened. We used to really criticise ourselves and analyse ourselves to death why we didn't win something but never really celebrated the success of the things we were winning. But the whole time our success rate has been very, very high. We can drive ourselves more effectively by selling the positive stories rather than trying to kick people in the behind with the negative stories, which is how we tended to operate in the past.

WJ: What impact has doing that had on the company?
JH: A big impact. One of the problems you have with an organisation like us is we have a pretty big market share, we talk about the 'Big Four' in our sector but we are way ahead of the other three. So if you're not careful there's going to be complacency so our focus has to be on how we can avoid complacency. In the past it used to be more the kick from behind rather than the carrot out in front. And that's really been quite a shift in mindset in that regard. We do drive ourselves and our people very hard and if you're not careful that can tip people over to being negative and de-motivating.

So by focusing on the successes and letting people see that there are still a number of success opportunities out there we've managed to achieve sustained growth for a period, and a pretty strong employment brand that people want to work with.

We also share stories via the 'PW-Scene', which is a monthly circular that goes out electronically telling the story about key events during the month. It's effective and we can monitor how many people are accessing it. The stories come from a wide range and we've got one of our marketing people who is dedicated to running it. Good stories tend to be passed on. We've got a couple of things that go on within the firm to keep the relationships close, a lot of reputations are built on those and the stories told of those events. For example we have quite a number of sports teams competing in different corporate leagues and dragon boat racing and people doing Rotorua marathons and the London marathon and lots of that sort of thing happening, which provides quite a good bit of storytelling. This is shared in that publication so people are aware that we're not just about keeping the clients happy. That's quite an important part of the employment brand so people are not just looking for a job to get a good experience, they want other things to be happening as well.

Interview with Brent Impey
CEO of MediaWorks

This was one of the last interviews Brent Impey did as CEO of MediaWorks New Zealand. MediaWorks NZ operates two national television channels (TV3 and C4) and radio stations out of 23 markets. Brent was appointed as CEO in 2000 and prior to that practised as a lawyer, specialising in media law. He has had a long association with the media, including previously being a director of several radio companies, Executive Director of the Radio Broadcasters' Association and its predecessor the Independent Broadcasters' Association. He has also acted as Chair of the Fred Hollows Foundation in New Zealand for the past 12 years.

WJ: How do you as an individual and as an organisation use storytelling?
BI: We use it here all the time. This whole business is about telling stories and yarns. For example yesterday we did for our new staff for television an orientation day, which involves about 10 or 12 of us, whether it's Mark Jennings, Head of News, or journalist and presenter Mike McRoberts or the heads of the various departments, getting up and talking about what they do so people know more about what the business is about. Mike was talking about his experiences in Beirut and the time they'd just got the word that the building they were in was going to get bombed. Or more recently he was meeting with the New Zealand Army platoon in Northern Afghanistan. I tell stories too. Because I have such a history with this place a lot of it is going back. What I might think is pretty boring, in fact some people find it quite interesting. Like how TV3 got its license, and telling stories about how

we fought 20 years ago when I was the company's lawyer to get the licence. And how I then came back eight or nine years later as the chief executive.

A lot of it is institutional knowledge that you use stories for because there are so many and a lot of situations repeat themselves. An example is the way in which the Tony Veitch story unfolded for TVNZ, one of their presenters charged with physical abuse and how they handled it. A lot of it relates to how you have your own experiences. We had our presenter Clint Brown who was charged with assault down in Taupo. It was interesting to observe how we handled that one and how they handled the one on Veitch, and whether you have the capacity to learn from these experiences and talk about them. We feel that they handled that completely wrongly by bringing him in, briefing him and then getting themselves involved and then walking away. You're either in or you're out. You use experiences to tell stories to help you run the business.

I don't believe in visions or mission statements. They had them here when I came here and I think they're rubbish. Because people sit around in a room and they dream up a vision for the business and then they come up with a mission statement that nobody ever reads. What we do here is essentially we sell advertising and then around it we build things around which we can sell advertising. If you really cut it back to what is done here we flog spots, and how do we do that? We go and convince people that we can give them a return by trusting us with their advertising dollars. The only way you can convince people to trust you with their advertising is by telling them a story about who and what you are, successes and failures you've had, being positive and being humble. When I do my presentation to orientation, which is an adaptation of other presentations, it's about that. It is that this business is about entrusting confidence in the advertising. To get that you've got to have listeners and viewers. And to get that you need a quality product. Linked into all of this is that I encourage people to be innovative and to take risks. The ringtone on my phone is Kenny Rogers 'The Gambler'. You've got to know when to hold and when to fold, that's what it's about. It's about doing deals and you can't do a deal with somebody who doesn't want to talk to you or doesn't want anything to do with you. So how do you do that? You gain their confidence.

WJ: What guides people in this organisation?
BI: We have objectives, staff development and a company philosophy.

Another part of all of this is it's got to be fun. This is a privilege to work in this sort of business where you get up every day and make or sell stuff, and enjoy yourself. It's not as if you're the oncology ward up at Auckland Hospital.

There are some things that are quite engrained. There are 1,100 staff, 440 in television and just under 700 in radio and we don't have a Human Resources department. This is because I don't believe in them. I believe that managers are taught to manage, you teach managers to manage people. We put a lot of resources into helping people who want to get into management to manage people. The radio people have training sessions every couple of months that bring the managers all together, and we'll bring in outside people to talk. And it's the same in television. If they can't manage people then it's my job to help them.

WJ: So you see it as your role rather than an HR role?
BI: Absolutely. I can't stand these situations where someone's working for a manager and it doesn't work out and the manager goes to the HR department and says, 'Can you get rid of Joey, because Joey's a tosser'. You've got to be the one to talk to Joey, he might have some things to say back to you. I tell a story where I describe a guy who I worked for in London who was Jewish and who married a Gentile and was excommunicated from his family. I hadn't really experienced any of this before. He had these superb negotiating skills to negotiate his way back into his family, which was a very strict Jewish family. I worked for this guy and his negotiating skills were unbelievable. It was always about leaving something on the table as you get no real benefit from screwing the guy to the last. I've carried that philosophy through. When you operate in a town like this you've got to. I tell that story about the Jew and the Gentile to my managers. I also say things like, 'It's my view that no idea is any good at all unless you can write it down and you can measure it.' And how did I get to that view? In my early legal days I worked for a guy named Brad Giles. He was a guy who got himself up from the bottom, from a poor home in Tauranga. He paid for his way through university and eventually became a judge. He was a fantastic judge and his motto was 'Get it down in writing', no matter how bad it is. If you get it in writing you can shape it from there. I use stories all the time by sharing some of my life experiences with my managers.

WJ: Do you have a formal structure for sharing stories?

BI: We have 'Telly Tales', which is a weekly newsletter from television that goes to every staff member through email and for radio we do a thing called 'The Week That Was' each week. It gives an update about what's happening and every quarter we put out a magazine. The stories in it are important as it's the culture of the place. Culture is a combination of history, events, how the business reacts under pressure, the dynamics of the place and the people, all of these things.

It's all about communication. The trick is to make sure that people within the organisation know everything there is to know about the organisation before people on the outside. I'll give you an example. One of our producers, Carol Hirschfield, resigned yesterday to go to Maori Television. We make sure that we've spoken to Maori TV. Press releases are expected to go out at 4pm and our staff know by 4pm too. That way they know about it before it becomes a public release. It's all about managing the communication, which is important because people have a pride in the place. The worst way to destroy pride is with one of their mates from the opposition ringing up and saying to them, 'You've lost Carol'.

WJ: How do you use storytelling outside the organisation?

BI: Mainly they're business-related, in terms of clients, advertisers, and our on-air broadcasters who are telling stories to their listeners and radio audience. Entertainment and breakfast radio is all about that. Long gone are the days where you took a joke book out and announced the latest joke. It's all about what's happening in your life right now. They talk to us about whether you buy free-range pork or not.

WJ: What benefits have you seen with using storytelling?

BI: I think that there's a view generally within our television and radio companies that we are the underdog competing against the establishment so we like to share stories of our success. This develops a 'can-do' attitude. The new creative director for television came from TVNZ and he said he can't believe how much he's done here on so little, and that's just the way it is. That's good; it permeates around the building and out. The key in this game is to get the best staff, and to get the best staff you've got to know that they want to come and work here. The employer of choice is what it comes down to.

WJ: Do you use storytelling in your presentations?

BI: I'm always telling stories. Like the yarns about the early days of private radio, or some personality stories about people walking out and throwing chairs out through windows and all those legendary sort of stories. I did an internal presentation recently where I was given 20 questions to answer as part of a training day for general managers and sales managers of radio. Questions were given to me the night before and ranged from: 'What is our biggest opportunity?' and 'What has been my greatest challenge?', right through to 'Who would I turn gay for?'. It's all about stories. Instead of getting up and doing a presentation, it is training through me telling them stuff that they otherwise wouldn't know and in a different way. There was a questioner who asked the questions and I just went from there, which meant it could be made entertaining. Humour is important in all these things. If it's humorous, people are more likely to remember it. It's such a valuable tool. There's nothing worse than sitting through a presentation by someone who's dry. You never read a PowerPoint; it's just a tool. There's much more power in stories.

Interview with David Pearce
CEO of CanTeen

David Pearce has been CEO of CanTeen since the beginning of 2009. Prior to that his professional career has been mainly in senior management positions in human resources and communication roles for large multinational companies such as Unilever and Fonterra, which has taken him around the world. CanTeen is a New Zealand organisation dedicated to ensuring no young person in New Zealand living with cancer should ever have to feel alone. It develops and empowers young people living with cancer through a national peer support network, and professional educational and recreational programmes.

WJ: What are the benefits of storytelling?
DP: I find that audiences seem to connect better, that the public and employees and members of organisations are tired of conventional communication and it doesn't sort of resonate. Most people seem to be able to empathise and connect with the story and so if I am tempted to put up a whole bunch of numbers of a whole lot of data for an argument, I may or may not connect, but if I start with a story I'm probably going to get your attention to begin with. I personalise that, but I'm finding it to be true of almost everyone. I'm finding it more both as a member of an audience and as someone who stands on stage. I'm finding that storytelling just gets a better response. You've got an audience buying in and maybe from there you could launch on to a persuasive argument or sharing of information, but it's the story which has perhaps warmed them to you to begin with.

WJ: Have you had any recent successes with that?

DP: Yesterday I went to a fairly large New Zealand-wide organisation who had selected us as the beneficiary for an annual donation. I met the Managing Director and it was clear he didn't know much about us. He said the staff had chosen us as they had decided to do an annual giving, rather than presents. He asked the staff to tell him what non-profit organisation they wanted to give all the money they would otherwise have spent on Christmas cards, staff gifts, etc. They chose CanTeen apparently hands down and I went along as the Managing Director wanted to know about CanTeen. I just took two photos of our people on our programmes and essentially I told him where his money would go. I talked about the young people from CanTeen, their lives, what happens at these programmes and how they benefited from it. I used real stories that I knew were true, I didn't name names, but I was able to talk about real-life examples. He was warmed, and interested immediately. He pulled his chair forward and it was one of the conversations I thought that was going to last five minutes but it was 20 minutes because he was engaged and he asked a lot of questions following the stories. He said he was genuinely interested to hear the stories about our members so I told him stories of our members' growth, their personal development, the trust and honesty that surfaces from these programmes. I told him a sad one about losing a member, one of the folks in the picture. I told him about a sibling story, I told him about a patient story, and he just loved them.

In the 20 minutes there was only one statistic and that was about the global rate of young people with cancer. It wasn't about numbers, it wasn't about dollars, it was about real people's stories. He was so interested that at the end of it he said, 'This is fantastic', he wanted to do more with this, and on the spot he came up with a strategy that would help us raise our profile nationwide. He just came up with that because he was so enthusiastic about CanTeen. I believe I have won another friend, and as it happens a friend in a very influential position of a giant media organisation with a national footprint. And it was simply because he was just taken with the wonderful stories of our members.

WJ: How do others use storytelling in the organisation?

DP: All our members have their own story. When we go to a high school or to a sponsor organisation, they don't particularly want to know about us, they actually want to know about the real people. So we get a young member to stand and tell them their story, their relationship with cancer; how I got cancer when I was 13 or my brother died of cancer when I was 17 or whatever it is. They just tell a relatively brief story about their brush with cancer and how they dealt with it, some of the highs and the lows.

We call it their member story and it tends to be their go-to when they have speaking engagements. Somewhere in New Zealand probably every day, someone's going to do a talk. Most of our 100 or so member leaders will be our regular speakers. We do coach them to tell their own story. We don't put words in their mouth, we don't script them, we help them to talk about their cancer journey in their own way, what they have learned, what they have gained from their participation in CanTeen and it's generally enough to win the audience. Storytelling works so well for us to help the public understand who we are, to help the public and sponsors get closer to us and frankly without overdoing the sympathy card, because we don't overplay that, but by telling our members' stories, for the public and sponsors, it becomes pretty easy for them to understand that these young people deserve and warrant our support.

WJ: Does storytelling play any other role in your organisation?
DP: The other thing we use stories for in CanTeen where it's not about winning the public over or having ourselves understood, is how we bring our values to life inside CanTeen. We're a geographically dispersed organisation with 1,333 members at the moment. We use storytelling to make CanTeen a smaller place, to give ourselves some things in common. So the hero stories, the values stories, means that if you go to the branch in Invercargill they'll have the same take on our values like 'Own It' or 'Do it Right' or 'Respect', as the Auckland branch members, because they have heard some of the same stories. It's not all rote; it's not all without variation but there are local stories and national folkloric stories but it works so much better than other forms of communication. You always see values posters hanging in receptions in the organisation you go to, mission statements and so forth, but I would argue the values are as well alive in CanTeen as in anywhere I have ever worked.

When I talk to our major sponsor and present their management development programmes and I want to talk about values, I'll share a story, a member's story about a value. We've got them all round New Zealand at every branch. If you were interviewing a staff member and you said, 'Tell me a story about a value', they'll tell you a real story that they've seen with their own eyes.

WJ: Can you share a story of one of your values in action?
DP: There are some stories you get told inside your organisation that become sort of folklore and you hear many people telling that same story. It might not be about them, it might be about a colleague. We have one about our previous president and chairman, 25-year-old Matt Truman. Matt is 90% blind and was at our national camp in Gore nearly two years ago. We have a lot of outdoor adventure activities as part of our national camp. And Matt would not have been able to see them but he's hearing a lot of laughter coming from up in the hills above him and he's wondering what's going on. He makes his way quite carefully up to the top of the hill and he's hearing all this giggling and yahooing and as he gets close to them he's probably able to see a bit of movement but probably not really know what's going on. But he comes to realise that what these guys are doing is they have got a whole bunch of mountain bikes and they're doing a downhill dirt track event down the side of a hill.

Matt being Matt, who's a pretty adventurous guy, wants a part of that but a blind guy going flat out down a hill, well, there's quite a risk there for danger and injury. The story he tells is everyone lined up down the side of the hill in a sort of trail about six foot apart like a railway track and they've put him on the bike and they're letting him go and they all basically stood there like bouncy bars and pushed him back up as he wobbled. He wobbled his way with some ups and downs, he got his way down the hill, and there's a photo of this young guy with a bloody great smile on his face. He's got a helmet on and he's going down a hill and he's trusted his teammates that he's not going to fall over because they're there for him. He can probably only see a few feet in front of him and he's just making out shapes of people but he knows they're there for him and he trusted them to be there for him.

Matt recounts that story, he's been telling it probably every week since, for the last two years, but he believed it was so typical of CanTeen, it shows the benefits of CanTeen for him, and the people with cancer were there for him. CanTeen has a mission statement that no young person dealing with cancer will ever have to go through that alone. It's essentially about peer support as a huge source of strength and confidence. Matt feels that the metaphor of going down that hill was such an obvious example of that peer support. He had this fantastic adventure that many people would have actually thought was beyond the blind guy, but it was possible because of the trust and support that he had from probably around 70 young CanTeen members. I've heard him tell it so many times that now others are telling that story about him. I have heard many people tell Matt's story. 'One Team' is one of our values and when you're trying to convey to new members what does One Team really mean, tell that story and what it meant to Matt. It beats the hell out of a PowerPoint.

WJ: Do you think it is easier to have those kinds of value stories in action in an organisation like CanTeen rather than the corporate organisations?
DP: I believe we'll have more moving stories but our stories don't necessarily have to be all about life or death. We keep saying young people are not defined by cancer it's just part of what they're dealing with but they've got big, full lives in many respects. I've worked in a corporate environment and it's harder at times to achieve that. Sometimes there is a cynicism when someone launches into a story. But I personally feel if the storyteller ploughs on with enthusiasm and sincerity, the audience can always tell a genuine moment. The power of a true story always comes true in the passion of the presenter. So I believe that while CanTeen can tell some fantastic heart-warming stories, heroic stories are possible in a commercial world too, you just have to be credible about it and be accurate, not overeager. I think whether we've got cancer or a life-threatening disease or whether we're simply just trying to put out some high-quality cheese, we are all interesting people. I truly believe that. Every one of us is interesting and if we have the confidence to tell our story, I find that an audience will listen.

It's something about people, we like to hear each other's story. We'll be more successful if we tell it in an interesting way, but people like to hear each other's story. And if the leader in the corporate environment can then translate the 'so what' in the story, 'I'm sharing this story with you because it illustrates the following', it can work extremely well. Yes in CanTeen, it's kind of easier to do in some ways but it can work in the corporate environment and I've seen good leaders do that in organisations I've been a part of.

WJ: Can you give me an example of such a leadership story?

DP: I used to work for a large Anglo-Dutch multinational called Unilever, where I was a communication supporter to the Chief Executive. I used to be the guy that facilitated his international road shows. He would travel around the world meeting about 4,500 of his senior managers. This was an organisation of 265,000 staff so it was a big outfit. We would travel to 13 different locations where he would tell them about how the business was tracking and what the themes for the focus were for the coming year and so forth, and he would always tell a story. The one that I liked the best was a true story. Because the organisation was publicly listed, he would front Wall Street, the London Stock Exchange, and the business analysts of the world on a regular basis. He happened to make a mistake, which made him look pretty silly in the press. He basically gave a dividend batch to the shareholders and then only six months later, had to go and raise a whole lot more finance for a major acquisition. All the financial analysts claimed how he got that one wrong.

At his global road shows to his senior managers, he walks up on stage and everyone thinks he's going to do the PowerPoint moment. Indeed, he is going to do the PowerPoint moment, it's coming, but he's saying I want to introduce the elephant in the room. He says I know you're all sitting up there but I doubt anybody's going to have the courage to ask me this, so I'm going to ask me this. He then introduced himself and then interviewed himself as if he was a Wall Street journalist. He asked, 'Why the hell did you do this? Cause it is really distracting the organisation, people were still telling the story, six months later, God that seemed really dumb'. He would tell his story and he said you know what, 'I got it wrong, I just got it wrong. It was dumb in hindsight, it was absolutely dumb, I got it wrong. But guess what? Now I forgive myself and I have moved on so let's do that eh?' He told that story on stage around the world. And everyone would laugh and that's exactly what happened. They stopped talking about it and moved on. The acquisition later on went extremely well but he just put it on the table right out front and he did it in a little storytelling way. He used a little bit of theatre and interviewed himself.

It was very effective and what it did later on when he did open forums in Singapore or in Dubai or in South Africa, wherever we were, the staff present felt confident that they could ask him tricky questions because he'd been prepared to put one upfront. He'd been prepared to expose his own frailty right up front and so the open question sessions which in some occasions in corporate environments can be rather stumbling and stilted, quiet or trivial, people felt confident enough to level the big one. Telling stories to make a presentation more interesting and using a little bit of creative theatre are wonderful partners.

Appendix
How to become a
storytelling organisation

All the forces in the world are not so powerful as an idea whose time has come.

Victor Hugo

This appendix is relevant for two reasons, for the organisation as a whole to consider and specifically whether you want your business unit or team to incorporate storytelling as a leadership tool. It may not be the CEO who initially champions the idea of embracing storytelling, in fact in more cases it's not. Ideas that create big change in an organisation usually come from someone enthusiastic. It may be someone in the middle of the organisation and that person's passion is contagious until it is caught at the top and then embraced. It could just be your team that uses organisational storytelling to your advantage. Over time the results will speak for themselves and then the storytelling concept can filter throughout the organisation.

If you want your organisation to be a storytelling organisation then you must start by telling stories. There's no magic switch you can hit and voila, now everyone is using storytelling effectively. There are however, some basic steps you can follow.

1. Start by thinking where you'll use stories first
2. Craft your stories to suit that situation
3. Know your stories well

4. Practise the skills to develop the storytelling mindset and delivery
5. Tell your stories
6. Now tell them again!

Lead by example and others will follow. Step outside your comfort zone and into the unknown and see where it takes you.

You must be the change you wish to see in the world.

Mahatma Gandhi

Read through the interviews and see what the different leaders in the different organisations do. Aside from telling stories yourself, some of the different strategies include:
» Having online databases of stories that people can access and contribute to
» Having online newsletters that share stories organisation-wide
» Making a point to share success stories and tell stories at formal occasions
» Having the expectation that people will tell stories every time they present, coach and share information
» Teaching storytelling skills to the top leaders, so they can model the desired behaviour

» Using storytelling in training programs such as inductions
» Focusing on using storytelling for a specific part of the business eg: customer service
» Providing training for managers to improve their storytelling skills
» Having DVDs or online videos that capture stories and are made available to the staff

And this is just a starting point.

The best way to start your online database is to ask staff to submit stories. You may want to start by asking them to provide stories where they have seen the organisation's values (or whatever word is used) in action. Stories are the lifeblood of the organisation and there is so much collective knowledge among the staff that it makes sense to tap into that. Also when people leave the organisation get them to supply brief stories on what they have learnt working there, how they'd improve things, what they liked and disliked about their job. Don't miss the opportunity to capture that knowledge before it leaves your organisation altogether.

A multi-million dollar machine had broken down and all productivity had ground to a halt as a result. No matter what the engineers did they couldn't get the machine to go. The senior executive was at his wits' end and got the manager to call in an expert. The expert came and carefully inspected the entire machine. He reached into the bag that he had brought with him and took out a small hammer. He then hit one of the machine's valves. All of a sudden the machine roared back to life and everyone was overjoyed. The senior executive was very grateful and asked the expert to send in his invoice. The invoice came in and was for $10,000. The senior executive was outraged, complaining that the expert only did a few minutes work and asked for the bill to be itemised. The new itemised invoice was sent in by the expert and was broken down into the following:
Hitting the valve: $10.00
Knowing where to hit: $9,990.00

Look at the different areas of the business where you need to connect, engage, inspire and communicate to people and you'll see a need and opportunity for stories. As the Chinese proverb says, 'Talk doesn't cook rice' – you have to get among people in the organisation and start telling stories. Do that, and the rest is history.

Recommended Reading

Below is a selection of books for those who seek more illumination.

Armstrong, David, *Managing By Storying Around.* New York: Doubleday, 1992
>Stories used by an executive who uses them in his workplace on a daily basis. A great inspiration.

Booher, Dianna, *Speak with Confidence.* New York: McGraw-Hill, 2003
>A great book filled with almost 500 tips. If you read just one book on improving as a public speaker – make it this one.

Booker, Christopher, *The Seven Basic Plots.* London: Continuum, 2004
>An epic book that shows how there is a limited number of plots (yes, seven) and what makes each one work when it comes to storytelling.

Boyd, Brian, *On the Origins of Stories.* Cambridge: Belknap Press, 2009
>A book that shows why we tell stories from an evolutionary point of view and how storytelling sharpens social cognition, encourages co-operation and fosters creativity.

Denning, Stephen, *The Leader's Guide to Storytelling.* San Francisco: Jossey-Bass, 2005
>The big book of organisational storytelling theory. Not necessarily the easiest or quickest of reads but definitely one worth reading.

Hall, Richard, *Brilliant Presentation.* Great Britain: Pearson Education Limited, 2007
>This is a quick, easy read with some useful pointers on improving your presentations.

Johnstone, Keith, *Impro.* New York: Eyre Methuen, 1981

This book captures the spirit of improvisation and is a great starting point for those interested in this wonderful art form.

Loehr, Jim, *The Power of Story.* New York: Free Press, 2007

This book looks at how the stories you tell yourself impact on your physical and mental well-being.

Maguire, Jack, *The Power of Personal Storytelling.* New York: Jeremy P. Tarcher/Putnam, 1998

This book encourages you to develop your own stories and has great activities to aid you in doing just that.

McAdams, Dan, *The Stories We Live By.* New York: Guilford Press, 1993

A book on narrative psychology that can be hard-going in places but fascinating none-the-less.

Owen, Nick, *The Magic of Metaphor.* Carmarthen: Crown House, 2001

A collection of great stories that can be used for a variety of situations.

Owen, Nick, *More Magic of Metaphor.* Carmarthen: Crown House, 2004

More stories with a guide on how you can use them for leading, influencing and motivating.

Simmons, Annette, *The Story Factor.* New York: Basic Books, 2002

This is a must-read. It's informative with lots of great examples. Start here if you want to increase your understanding of organisational storytelling.

Taylor, Daniel, *The Healing Power of Stories.* New York: Doubleday, 1996

This book covers the importance of storytelling and its role in our mental, physical and emotional health. Highly recommended.

Yolen, Jane, *Favourite Folktales From Around the World.* New York: Pantheon Books, 1986

A wonderful collection of folktales that make for great reading, for adult and child alike.

About the Author

Wade Jackson is a wearer of many hats. One hat sees him as an international speaker and consultant on self-intelligence, creativity, and organisational storytelling. Another hat sees him travelling the world as a performer, director, teacher and producer of the art of improvisation. Other hats see him as an author and co-creator of the critically acclaimed JOLT Challenge program, working as a hypnotherapist and starring on stage and screen as an actor and improv comedian.

Wade is a playwright, an award-winning theatre producer, is fluent in Japanese, and holds three internationally recognised black belts in martial arts. His sense of adventure has taken him around the world, where he has studied the performing, healing and martial arts with masters in their fields and he integrates his diverse background into everything that he does. From these different art forms he brings together a unique combination of tools and strategies to help people transform their personal and professional lives.

A master storyteller, Wade has been teaching narrative for over 16 years. As a speaker and consultant, Wade has worked internationally with thousands of people ranging from CEOs, senior executive teams, Universities, Militaries and not-for-profit organisations. Clients who have engaged his services include Air New Zealand, American Express, AMP, Deloitte, Estée Lauder, National Australia Bank, Singapore Armed Forces and Vodafone to name a few. He is an honorary lecturer in Organisational Behaviour at AUT University, Faculty of Business and Law and is a faculty member of the New Zealand Institute of Management.

Wade is passionate about helping people live an authentic and purposeful life. You can contact him via his website: www.improvwarrior.com